Each Friday lesson consists of a writing prompt that directs students to write in response to the week's four-paragraph composition. This gives students the opportunity to apply the skills they have practiced during the week in their own writing. Students gain experience writing in a wide variety of forms, always with the support of familiar models.

## Friday writing prompts include:

- a prompt to write a composition in the same form as modeled in the weekly lesson

- sample topic sentences to support reluctant writers

- a weekly lesson identifier

Using the same voice as the previous writer, write one or two paragraphs that describe some of the things Marco Polo saw and the reaction of his neighbors. Begin with one of the following topic sentences, or write your own:

- Marco Polo returned recently from a 24-year adventure.
- Marco Polo claims to have seen many things during his journeys.
- I could listen all day to Marco Polo's stories about his travels.

**FRIDAY – WEEK 34**                    **Historical Fiction: Marco Polo's Tales**

Write one or two paragraphs describing Madagascar. Begin with one of the following topic sentences, or write your own:

- Madagascar is filled with wonderful things to see.
- Although it's just off the coast of Africa, the island of Madagascar is a world of its own.
- Madagascar is a fascinating country filled with many unique creatures and plants.

- hints to help students address skills that are specific to the writing form

- a label indicating the type of writing modeled in the weekly lesson

An Editing Checklist for students (see page 11) helps them revise their own writing or critique their peers' efforts. An Assessment Rubric (see page 9) is provided to help you assess student writing.

A reproducible student Language Handbook (pages 168–176) outlines the usage and mechanics rules for students to follow in editing the daily paragraphs. The Handbook includes examples to help familiarize students with how the conventions of language and mechanics are applied in authentic writing.

# How to Use *Daily Paragraph Editing*

You may use *Daily Paragraph Editing* in several ways, depending on your instructional objectives and your students' needs. Over time, you will probably want to introduce each of the presentation strategies outlined below so you can identify the approach that works best for you and your students.

The four paragraphs that comprise each week's editing lessons include a set of errors that are repeated throughout all four paragraphs. We recommend that you provide a folder for students to keep their *Daily Paragraph Editing* reference materials and weekly lessons. It will work best to reproduce and distribute all four daily paragraphs for a given week on Monday. That way, students can use the previous days' lessons for reference as the week progresses.

## Directed Group Lessons

*Daily Paragraph Editing* activities will be most successful if you first introduce them as a group activity. You might also have students edit individual copies of the day's lesson as you work through the paragraph with the group. Continue presenting the Monday through Thursday lessons to the entire class until you are confident that students are familiar with the editing process. Try any of the following methods to direct group lessons:

### Option 1

1. Create and display an overhead transparency of the day's paragraph.

2. Read the paragraph aloud just as it is written, including all the errors.

3. Read the paragraph a second time, using phrasing and intonation that would be appropriate if all end punctuation were correct. (You may find it helpful to read from the Editing Key.) Read all other errors as they appear in the text.

4. Guide students in correcting all end punctuation and initial capitals in the paragraph; mark corrections in erasable pen on the overhead transparency.

5. After the paragraph is correctly divided into sentences, review it one sentence at a time. Have volunteers point out errors as you come to them, and identify the necessary corrections. Encourage students to explain the reason for each correction; explain or clarify any rules that are unfamiliar.

EMC 2729 • Daily Paragraph Editing • ©2004 by Evan-Moor Corp.

## Option 2

Follow Steps 1–4 on page 4, and then work with students to focus on one type of error at a time, correcting all errors of the same type (i.e., capitalization, commas, subject/verb agreement, spelling, etc.) in the paragraph before moving on to another type. Refer to the Error Summary in the Editing Key to help you identify the various types of errors.

## Option 3

Use directed group lesson time to conduct a minilesson on one or more of the skills emphasized in that day's lesson. This is especially appropriate for new or unfamiliar skills, or for skills that are especially challenging or confusing for students. After introducing a specific skill, use the approach outlined in Option 2 to focus on that skill in one or more of the week's daily paragraphs. To provide additional practice, refer to the Skills Scope & Sequence to find other paragraphs that include the same target skill.

## Individual Practice

Once students are familiar with the process for editing the daily paragraphs, they may work on their own or with a partner to make corrections. Be sure students have their Proofreading Marks available to help them mark their corrections. Remind students to refer to the student Language Handbook as needed for guidance in the rules of mechanics and usage. Some students may find it helpful to know at the outset the number and types of errors they are seeking. Provide this information by referring to the Error Summary on the annotated Editing Key pages. You may wish to use a transparency on the overhead to check work with the group. Occasionally, you may wish to assess students' acquisition of skills by collecting and reviewing their work before they check it.

## Customizing Instruction

Some of the skills covered in *Daily Paragraph Editing* may not be part of the grade-level expectancies in the language program you use. Some skills may even be taught differently in your program from the way they are modeled in *Daily Paragraph Editing*. In such cases, follow the approach used in your program. Simply revise the paragraph text as needed by covering it with correction fluid or by writing in changes before you reproduce copies for students.

Comma usage is an area where discrepancies are most likely to arise. *Daily Paragraph Editing* uses the "closed" style, where commas are included after short introductory phrases. Except for commas used in salutations, closings, dates, and between city and state in letters, journals, or news articles, all commas that appear in the daily paragraphs have been correctly placed according to the closed style. All other skills related to the use of commas are practiced by requiring students to insert missing commas, rather than moving or deleting extraneous commas.

Occasionally, you or your students may make a correction that differs from that shown in the Editing Key. The decision to use an exclamation mark instead of a period, or a period instead of a semicolon, is often a subjective decision made by individual writers. When discrepancies of this sort arise, capitalize on the "teachable moment" to let students know that there are gray areas in English usage and mechanics, and discuss how each of the possible correct choices can affect the meaning or tone of the writing.

You may wish to have your students mark corrections on the daily paragraphs in a manner that differs from the common proofreading marks on page 10. If so, model the marking style you wish students to follow as you conduct group lessons on an overhead, and point out any differences between the standard proofing marks and those to be used by your students.

## Using the Writing Prompts

Have students keep their daily paragraphs in a folder so they can review the week's four corrected paragraphs on Friday. Identify the type of writing modeled in the four-paragraph composition and any of its special features (e.g., dialog in a fictional narrative; salutation, closing, and paragraph style in a letter; opinion statements and supporting arguments in an editorial; etc.).

Present the Friday writing prompt on an overhead transparency, write it on the board, or distribute individual copies to students. Take a few minutes to brainstorm ideas with the group and to focus on language skills that students will need to address in their writing.

After students complete their writing, encourage them to use the Editing Checklist (see page 11) to review or revise their work. You may also wish to have partners review each other's writing. To conduct a more formal assessment of students' writing, use the Assessment Rubric on page 9.

If you assign paragraph writing for homework, be sure students have the week's four corrected paragraphs available as a reference. You may wish to set aside some time for volunteers to read their completed writing to the class, or display compositions on a weekly writing bulletin board for students to enjoy.

# Skills Scope and Sequence

## Capitalization

| Skill | 1 | 2 | 3 | 4 | 5 | 6 | 7 | 8 | 9 | 10 | 11 | 12 | 13 | 14 | 15 | 16 | 17 | 18 | 19 | 20 | 21 | 22 | 23 | 24 | 25 | 26 | 27 | 28 | 29 | 30 | 31 | 32 | 33 | 34 | 35 | 36 |
|---|---|---|---|---|---|---|---|---|---|---|---|---|---|---|---|---|---|---|---|---|---|---|---|---|---|---|---|---|---|---|---|---|---|---|---|---|
| Beginning of Sentences, Quotations, Salutations/Closings | • |  | • | • | • | • | • | • | • | • | • | • | • | • | • | • | • | • | • | • |  | • | • | • | • | • | • | • | • | • | • |  |  | • | • | • |
| Days & Months |  |  |  |  | • |  |  |  |  | • | • |  |  | • |  | • |  |  |  |  | • | • |  |  |  |  |  |  |  |  |  |  | • |  |  |  |
| Holidays |  |  |  |  |  |  |  |  |  | • |  |  |  |  |  |  | • |  |  |  |  |  |  |  |  |  |  |  |  |  |  |  |  |  |  | • |
| Incorrect Use of Capitals | • |  | • |  | • | • | • | • | • | • | • | • | • | • | • | • | • | • | • | • | • | • | • | • | • | • | • | • | • | • | • | • | • | • | • | • |
| Names & Titles of People, incl. Languages, Nationalities | • | • | • | • |  | • | • | • | • |  |  | • |  |  |  |  |  | • |  |  |  |  |  | • |  | • |  | • |  |  |  | • | • | • |  | • |
| Names of Places, Special Things, Organizations (including abbreviations) | • | • |  | • |  |  | • |  | • |  |  |  |  | • |  |  |  |  | • |  |  |  |  |  |  |  |  |  |  |  | • |  | • | • | • |  |
| Nouns Used as Names (Aunt, Grandpa, etc.) |  |  |  |  |  |  |  |  |  |  |  |  |  |  |  | • |  |  |  |  |  |  |  |  |  | • |  |  |  |  | • |  |  |  |  |  |
| Titles of Books, Magazines, Poems, Stories |  |  | • |  |  |  |  |  |  |  |  |  |  |  |  |  |  |  |  | • |  |  |  | • |  |  |  | • |  |  |  |  |  |  |  | • |
| Titles of Movies, TV Shows, Songs |  |  |  |  |  |  |  |  | • |  |  |  |  |  |  |  |  |  |  |  |  |  |  |  |  |  |  |  | • |  |  |  |  |  |  |  |
| Word I |  |  |  |  | • |  |  |  |  |  |  |  |  |  | • |  |  |  |  |  |  |  |  |  |  |  |  |  |  |  | • | • | • | • | • |  |

## Language Usage

| Skill | 1 | 2 | 3 | 4 | 5 | 6 | 7 | 8 | 9 | 10 | 11 | 12 | 13 | 14 | 15 | 16 | 17 | 18 | 19 | 20 | 21 | 22 | 23 | 24 | 25 | 26 | 27 | 28 | 29 | 30 | 31 | 32 | 33 | 34 | 35 | 36 |
|---|---|---|---|---|---|---|---|---|---|---|---|---|---|---|---|---|---|---|---|---|---|---|---|---|---|---|---|---|---|---|---|---|---|---|---|---|
| Correct Use of Singular & Plural Forms | • | • |  |  | • | • | • | • | • | • | • | • | • | • |  |  | • |  | • | • |  | • | • |  | • | • | • | • | • |  |  |  |  | • | • | • |
| Correct Use of Verb Tenses | • |  | • | • | • | • | • | • | • | • | • | • | • | • | • | • | • | • | • | • | • | • | • | • | • | • | • | • | • |  | • | • | • |  | • | • |
| Identify Double Negatives |  |  |  |  |  |  |  | • |  | • |  |  |  |  |  |  |  |  |  |  |  |  |  |  |  |  |  |  |  |  |  |  |  |  |  | • |
| Use of Correct Adjective & Adverbial Forms |  |  | • | • |  | • | • | • | • | • | • | • | • | • | • | • | • |  | • |  |  |  | • | • | • |  | • | • |  | • | • | • | • | • |  |  |
| Use of Correct Pronouns | • |  |  |  |  |  |  |  |  |  |  |  |  |  |  |  |  |  |  |  |  |  |  |  |  |  |  |  |  |  |  | • |  | • |  |  |

## Punctuation: Apostrophes

| Skill | 1 | 2 | 3 | 4 | 5 | 6 | 7 | 8 | 9 | 10 | 11 | 12 | 13 | 14 | 15 | 16 | 17 | 18 | 19 | 20 | 21 | 22 | 23 | 24 | 25 | 26 | 27 | 28 | 29 | 30 | 31 | 32 | 33 | 34 | 35 | 36 |
|---|---|---|---|---|---|---|---|---|---|---|---|---|---|---|---|---|---|---|---|---|---|---|---|---|---|---|---|---|---|---|---|---|---|---|---|---|
| In Contractions | • | • |  | • | • | • | • | • | • | • | • | • | • | • | • | • | • | • | • | • | • | • | • | • | • | • | • | • | • | • | • | • | • | • | • | • |
| In Possessives | • |  | • | • | • | • | • | • | • | • | • | • | • | • | • |  | • | • | • | • | • | • | • | • | • | • | • | • | • | • | • | • | • | • | • | • |
| Improperly Placed | • |  | • |  | • |  |  | • |  |  |  |  |  | • |  |  |  |  |  |  |  |  |  |  | • |  |  |  | • |  |  |  |  |  |  |  |

## Punctuation: Commas

| Skill | 1 | 2 | 3 | 4 | 5 | 6 | 7 | 8 | 9 | 10 | 11 | 12 | 13 | 14 | 15 | 16 | 17 | 18 | 19 | 20 | 21 | 22 | 23 | 24 | 25 | 26 | 27 | 28 | 29 | 30 | 31 | 32 | 33 | 34 | 35 | 36 |
|---|---|---|---|---|---|---|---|---|---|---|---|---|---|---|---|---|---|---|---|---|---|---|---|---|---|---|---|---|---|---|---|---|---|---|---|---|
| After Introductory Dependent Phrase or Clause | • | • | • | • | • | • | • | • | • | • | • | • | • | • | • | • | • | • | • | • | • | • | • | • | • | • | • | • | • | • | • | • | • | • | • | • |
| After Introductory Interjection or Expression |  |  |  |  |  | • |  |  |  |  |  |  |  |  |  |  |  | • |  |  |  |  |  |  |  |  |  |  |  |  | • |  |  |  |  | • |
| After Salutation & Closing in a Letter |  |  |  | • |  |  |  |  |  | • |  |  |  |  |  |  |  |  |  |  |  |  |  |  |  |  |  |  |  |  |  |  |  |  |  |  |
| Between City & State & City & Country Names |  |  | • |  |  |  |  |  |  |  |  |  |  |  |  |  |  |  |  | • |  |  |  |  | • |  |  |  |  | • |  |  |  |  |  |  |
| Between Equally Modifying Adjectives |  |  | • | • |  | • |  |  |  |  |  |  |  |  |  |  |  |  |  | • |  |  |  |  |  |  |  |  |  |  |  |  |  |  |  |  |
| Between Items in a Series | • | • | • | • | • | • | • | • | • | • | • | • | • | • | • | • | • | • | • | • | • | • | • | • | • | • | • | • | • | • | • | • | • | • | • | • |
| In a Date |  |  |  |  |  |  |  |  |  |  |  |  |  |  |  | • |  |  |  |  |  | • |  |  |  |  |  |  |  |  |  |  | • |  |  |  |
| To Separate Parts of Compound Sentences | • | • | • | • | • | • | • | • | • | • | • | • | • | • | • | • | • | • | • | • | • | • | • | • | • | • | • | • | • | • | • | • | • | • | • | • |
| To Set Off Appositives | • | • |  | • | • |  |  |  |  |  |  |  |  |  |  |  | • |  |  |  |  |  | • |  |  |  |  |  |  |  |  |  |  | • | • | • |
| To Set Off Interruptions | • |  |  | • |  |  |  |  |  |  |  |  |  |  |  | • |  |  |  |  |  |  |  |  |  |  |  | • |  |  |  |  |  |  | • | • |
| To Set Off Quotations |  |  | • |  |  |  |  |  | • |  |  |  |  |  |  |  |  |  |  |  |  |  |  |  |  |  |  |  |  |  |  |  | • |  |  | • |
| With Name Used in Direct Address |  |  |  |  |  |  |  |  |  |  |  |  |  |  |  |  |  |  |  |  |  |  |  |  |  |  |  |  |  |  | • | • |  | • |  |  |

# Skills Scope and Sequence (continued)

Week No.

| Skill | 1 | 2 | 3 | 4 | 5 | 6 | 7 | 8 | 9 | 10 | 11 | 12 | 13 | 14 | 15 | 16 | 17 | 18 | 19 | 20 | 21 | 22 | 23 | 24 | 25 | 26 | 27 | 28 | 29 | 30 | 31 | 32 | 33 | 34 | 35 | 36 |
|---|---|---|---|---|---|---|---|---|---|---|---|---|---|---|---|---|---|---|---|---|---|---|---|---|---|---|---|---|---|---|---|---|---|---|---|---|
| **Punctuation: Periods** | | | | | | | | | | | | | | | | | | | | | | | | | | | | | | | | | | | | |
| After Initials | | | | | | | | | | • | | | | | | | | | | | | | | | | | | | • | | | | | | | • |
| At End of Sentence | • | • | • | • | • | • | • | • | • | • | • | • | • | • | • | • | • | | • | • | • | • | • | • | • | • | • | • | • | • | • | • | • | • | • | • |
| In Time & Measurement Abbreviations | | | | | | | | | | | • | | • | | | | | | • | | | | | | • | | • | | | | | • | | | | |
| In Title Abbreviations | | | | | | | | | | | | | | | | | | | | | | | | • | | | | | | | | • | | | | |
| To Correct Run-on & Rambling Sentences; Fragments | • | • | • | | | | | | | | | • | | • | • | | | • | | • | | | | | | • | | | | | • | | • | | | |
| **Punctuation: Quotation Marks** | | | | | | | | | | | | | | | | | | | | | | | | | | | | | | | | | | | | |
| In Speech | | • | | | • | • | | | • | • | | • | | | • | • | | | | | | • | | | • | | | • | | • | | | • | • | | • |
| To Set Apart Special Words | | | • | • | • | • | | • | | | | | | | | | | | | | • | | | | • | | | • | | | • | | • | • | • | • |
| With Titles of Works of Art, Articles, Poems, Chapters, Short Stories, Songs, Newspaper Articles | | | | | | | | | • | | | | | | | | | | | • | | | | • | | | | • | | • | | | | | | |
| **Punctuation: Other** | | | | | | | | | | | | | | | | | | | | | | | | | | | | | | | | | | | | |
| Colon in Time | | | | | | | | | | | | | • | | | | | | | | | | | | | | | | | | | • | | | | |
| Exclamation Point | | | | | | | | | | | | | | | | | • | | | | | • | | | | | | | | | | | • | | | |
| Hyphen in Fractions | | | | • | | | | | | | | | | | | | | | | | | | | | | | | | | | | | | • | | |
| Hyphen to Form Adjectives | | | | | | | | | | • | | | | • | | | | | | | | | | | | | | | | | | | | • | • | |
| Periods & Commas Inside Quotation Marks | | | | | • | | | | | | | • | | • | • | | | | | | • | | | • | | • | | • | | • | • | • | • | | | • |
| Question Mark | • | • | | • | • | • | • | | • | | | | | | | • | | | | | | • | | | | | | | | | • | • | • | | | • |
| Semicolon to Join Two Independent Clauses | | | | | | | | | | | | | | | | | | | | | | | | | | | | | | | | | • | | | • |
| Underline Names of Aircraft & Ships | | | | | | | | | | | | | | | | | | | | | | | | | | | | | | | | | • | | | |
| Underline Titles of Books, Magazines, Movies, Newspapers, TV Shows | | | • | | | | | | | | | | | | | | | | | | | | | • | | | | • | | | | | | | | |
| **Spelling** | | | | | | | | | | | | | | | | | | | | | | | | | | | | | | | | | | | | |
| Identify Errors in Grade-Level Words | • | • | • | • | • | • | • | • | • | • | • | • | • | • | • | • | • | • | • | • | • | • | • | • | • | • | • | • | • | • | • | • | • | • | • | • |

8

## Assessment Rubric for Evaluating Friday Paragraph Writing

The Friday writing prompts give students the opportunity to use the capitalization, punctuation, and other usage and mechanics skills that have been practiced during the week's editing tasks. They also require students to write in a variety of different forms and genres.

In evaluating students' Friday paragraphs, you may wish to focus exclusively on their mastery of the aspects of mechanics and usage targeted that week. However, if you wish to conduct a more global assessment of student writing, the following rubric offers broad guidelines for evaluating the composition as a whole.

# Characteristics of Student Writing

| | EXCELLENT | GOOD | FAIR | WEAK |
|---|---|---|---|---|
| **Clarity and Focus** | Writing is exceptionally clear, focused, and interesting. | Writing is generally clear, focused, and interesting. | Writing is loosely focused on the topic. | Writing is unclear and unfocused. |
| **Development of Main Ideas** | Main ideas are clear, specific, and well-developed. | Main ideas are identifiable, but may be somewhat general. | Main ideas are overly broad or simplistic. | Main ideas are unclear or not expressed. |
| **Organization** | Organization is clear (beginning, middle, and end) and fits the topic and writing form. | Organization is clear, but may be predictable or formulaic. | Organization is attempted, but is often unclear. | Organization is not coherent. |
| **Use of Details** | Details are relevant, specific, and well-placed. | Details are relevant, but may be overly general. | Details may be off-topic, predictable, or not specific enough. | Details are absent or insufficient to support main ideas. |
| **Vocabulary** | Vocabulary is exceptionally rich, varied, and well-chosen. | Vocabulary is colorful and generally avoids clichés. | Vocabulary is ordinary and may rely on clichés. | Vocabulary is limited, general, or vague. |
| **Mechanics and Usage** | Demonstrates exceptionally strong command of conventions of punctuation, capitalization, spelling, and usage. | Demonstrates control of conventions of punctuation, capitalization, spelling, and usage. | Errors in use of conventions of mechanics and usage distract, but do not impede, the reader. | Limited ability to control conventions of mechanics and usage impairs readability of the composition. |

# Proofreading Marks

Use these marks to show corrections.

| Mark | Meaning | Example |
|------|---------|---------|
| ℘ | Take this out (delete). | I love ~~to~~ to read. |
| ⊙ | Add a period. | It was late⊙ |
| ≡ | Make this a capital letter. | First prize went to <u>maria</u>. |
| / | Make this a lowercase letter. | We saw a ~~B~~lack ~~C~~at. |
| —— | Fix the spelling. | This is our ~~hause~~ house. |
| ∧ | Add a comma. | Goodnight∧Mom. |
| ∨ | Add an apostrophe. | It∨s mine. |
| ∨ ∨ | Add quotation marks. | ∨Come in,∨ he said. |
| !∧ ?∧ | Add an exclamation point or a question mark. | Help!∧Can you help me?∧ |
| ∧̄ | Add a hyphen. | Let's go in∧̄line skating after school. |
| ‿ | Close the space. | Foot‿ball is fun. |
| ∧ | Add a word. | The∧pen is mine. red |
| —— | Underline the words. | We read <u>Old Yeller</u>. |
| ⨨ ⨨ | Add a semicolon or a colon. | Alex arrived at 400∧Debbie came later. |

EMC 2729 • Daily Paragraph Editing • ©2004 by Evan-Moor Corp.

**Editing Checklist**

Use this checklist to review and revise your writing:

- ◯ Does each sentence begin with a capital letter?

- ◯ Do names of people and places begin with a capital letter?

- ◯ Does each sentence end with a period, a question mark, or an exclamation point?

- ◯ Did I use apostrophes to show possession (*Ana's desk*) and in contractions (*isn't*)?

- ◯ Did I choose the correct word (*to, too, two*)?

- ◯ Did I check for spelling errors?

- ◯ Did I place commas where they are needed?

- ◯ Are my sentences clear and complete?

**Editing Checklist**

Use this checklist to review and revise your writing:

- ◯ Does each sentence begin with a capital letter?

- ◯ Do names of people and places begin with a capital letter?

- ◯ Does each sentence end with a period, a question mark, or an exclamation point?

- ◯ Did I use apostrophes to show possession (*Ana's desk*) and in contractions (*isn't*)?

- ◯ Did I choose the correct word (*to, too, two*)?

- ◯ Did I check for spelling errors?

- ◯ Did I place commas where they are needed?

- ◯ Are my sentences clear and complete?

Preview the 4 daily lessons to ensure you review or introduce skills that may be unfamiliar to students.

# A Sticky Business

Did you know that the chewing gum industry is more than just a sticky business? it also earns millions of dollars. The united states produces about 24,000,000 miles of chewing gum each year gum is available in different varieties flavors and shapes but did you ever wonder where wear gum comes from? Did you ever wonder how it's made and where and when the first people began to chew it? People have been chewing gum it turns out for a very long time.

**Error Summary**

| | |
|---|---|
| Capitalization | 4 |
| Punctuation: | |
|   Apostrophe | 1 |
|   Comma | 5 |
|   Period | 2 |
|   Other | 3 |
| Spelling | 1 |

**MONDAY**      **WEEK 1**

more than a thousand years ago the mayans and other peoples of central america chewed chicle. Chicle is the hardened sap of the sapodilla tree ancient greeks we're chewing gum made from the sap of the mastic tree. the native americans of north america were chewing gum made from spruce sap. By the early 1800s the first store to make and sell spruce gum had opened in north america. in the 1860s, the use of chicle as a chewing gum was developed and gums popularity began to raise rise.

**Error Summary**

| | |
|---|---|
| Capitalization | 14 |
| Language Usage | 1 |
| Punctuation: | |
|   Apostrophe | 1 |
|   Comma | 3 |
|   Period | 2 |
| Spelling | 1 |

**TUESDAY**      **WEEK 1**

EMC 2729 • Daily Paragraph Editing, Grade 6 • ©2004 by Evan-Moor Corp.

Name _____

# A Sticky Business

Did you know that the chewing gum industry is more than just a sticky business it also earns millions of dollars. The united states produces about 24,000,000 miles of chewing gum each year gum is available in different varieties flavors and shapes but did you ever wonder wear gum comes from Did you ever wonder how its made and where and when the first people began to chew it People have been chewing gum it turns out for a very long time

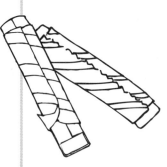

- commas
- question marks

**MONDAY**        **WEEK 1**

more than a thousand years ago the mayans and other peoples of central america chewed chicle. Chicle is the hardened sap of the sapodilla tree ancient greeks we're chewing gum made from the sap of the mastic tree. the native americans of north america were chewing gum made from spruce sap. By the early 1800s the first store to make and sell spruce gum had opened in north america. in the 1860s, the use of chicle as a chewing gum was developed and gums popularity began to raise

- commas
- names of places
- names of ethnic groups

**TUESDAY**        **WEEK 1**

Chicle-based gum was first manufactured as a result of a failed experiment antonio lopez de santa anna the mexican general whose army defeated the texans at the alamo in 1836 Brought chicle to new york in 1860. He hoped to sell it as a type of rubber a man named thomas adams ~~tryed~~ tried to make this "rubber" harden but he failed. Discovering instead that the rubber could be chewed Adams ~~adds~~ added flavorings. he began to ~~made~~ make gum with a chicle base

**Error Summary**

| | |
|---|---|
| Capitalization | 14 |
| Language Usage | 2 |
| Punctuation: | |
| Comma | 4 |
| Period | 3 |
| Spelling | 1 |

**WEDNESDAY**　　　　**WEEK 1**

the main ingredient of chewing gum was chicle until the mid-1900s. today, gum bases are made from melted rubber waxes or plastics. After the gum base has been cleaned softeners sweeteners and flavorings ~~is~~ are added Chewing gum continues to sell and some surveys report that the average american chews 200 sticks of gum a year. some people chew gum for the taste but others chew it to help ~~him~~ them stay alert or to help them relax

**Error Summary**

| | |
|---|---|
| Capitalization | 4 |
| Language Usage | 2 |
| Punctuation: | |
| Comma | 7 |
| Period | 2 |

**THURSDAY**　　　　**WEEK 1**

Name _____

Chicle-based gum was first manufactured as a result of a failed experiment antonio lopez de santa anna the mexican general whose army defeated the texans at the alamo in 1836. Brought chicle to new york in 1860. He hoped to sell it as a type of rubber a man named thomas adams tryed to make this "rubber" harden but he failed. Discovering instead that the rubber could be chewed Adams adds flavorings. he began to made gum with a chicle base

- commas
- names of people
- names of places
- names of ethnic groups

**WEDNESDAY                                    WEEK 1**

the main ingredient of chewing gum was chicle until the mid-1900s. today, gum bases are made from melted rubber waxes or plastics. After the gum base has been cleaned softeners sweeteners and flavorings is added Chewing gum continues to sell and some surveys report that the average american chews 200 sticks of gum a year. some people chew gum for the taste but others chew it to help him stay alert or to help them relax

- commas
- names of ethnic groups

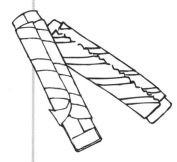

**THURSDAY                                     WEEK 1**

Preview the 4 daily lessons to ensure you review or introduce skills that may be unfamiliar to students.

# Scurvy

directions can some times be confusing and hard
to follow, but the directions for preventing scurvy ~~is~~ *are*
easy. Eat oranges, lemons, and other citrus fruits. What
is Scurvy? how does eating citrus fruit prevent scurvy?
Scurvy is a disease, That people get if they dont get
enough vitamin C. They become very weak, ~~there~~ *their* gums
become spongy and inflamed, and ~~they're~~ *their* teeth become
loose and may even fall out.

| Error Summary | |
|---|---|
| Capitalization | 4 |
| Language Usage | 1 |
| Punctuation: | |
|   Apostrophe | 1 |
|   Comma | 4 |
|   Period | 2 |
|   Other | 2 |
| Spelling | 3 |

**MONDAY**　　　　　　　　　　　　　**WEEK 2**

The directions seem simple today, but people
didnt know about Vitamins a long time ago. people
only knew that sailors began to die of this terrible
disease on long sea ~~journies.~~ *journeys* james cook, a famous
british navigator, was the first sea captain to prevent
scurvy in his men. Born in 1728, Cook ~~were~~ *was* the first
european to explore hawai`i and other parts of the
south pacific ocean he sailed to tahiti, new zealand,
and australia.

| Error Summary | |
|---|---|
| Capitalization | 15 |
| Language Usage | 1 |
| Punctuation: | |
|   Apostrophe | 1 |
|   Comma | 5 |
|   Period | 2 |
| Spelling | 1 |

**TUESDAY**　　　　　　　　　　　　　**WEEK 2**

Name _____

# Scurvy

directions can some times be confusing and hard to follow but the directions for preventing scurvy is easy. Eat oranges lemons and other citrus fruits. What is Scurvy. how does eating citrus fruit prevent scurvy Scurvy is a disease. That people get if they dont get enough vitamin C. They become very weak, there gums become spongy and inflamed and they're teeth become loose and may even fall out

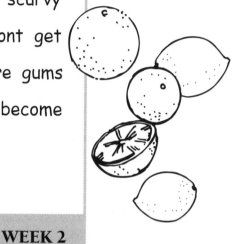

- question marks
- commas

**MONDAY**                                         **WEEK 2**

The directions seem simple today but people didnt know about Vitamins a long time ago. people only knew that sailors began to die of this terrible disease on long sea journies. james cook a famous british navigator was the first sea captain to prevent scurvy in his men. Born in 1728, Cook were the first european to explore hawai`i and other parts of the south pacific ocean he sailed to tahiti new zealand and australia

- commas
- names of people
- names of ethnic groups

**TUESDAY**                                         **WEEK 2**

Despite the length of Cook's expeditions, very few of his men died from scurvy. Cook was able to prevent scurvy in his men by stocking his ships with sauerkraut. Cook forced his men to eat it daily, and he made them eat fresh foods at port stops. At first, some sailors didn't want to follow Cook's dietary rules. It wasn't until 1795, sixteen years after Cook's death, that lime juice was issued to all british naval vessels. As a result, scurvy began to disappear among british seamen, just as it had with Cook's crews.

**Error Summary**

| | |
|---|---|
| Capitalization | 4 |
| Language Usage | 1 |
| Punctuation: | |
| Apostrophe | 6 |
| Comma | 3 |
| Period | 1 |

**WEDNESDAY**                    **WEEK 2**

We know today that Vitamin c, or ascorbic acid, is necessary for the formation of tendons, ligaments, bones, and cartilage. Vitamin c is found in lots of fresh foods, including oranges, lemons, and melons. It's also found in tomatoes, grapefruit, and bananas. Today, cases of scurvy are rare because it is easy to get fresh food. Captain cook didn't know what we do now about vitamins, but he made his men follow life-saving directions. With Cook's directions, scurvy, a deadly disease, was prevented.

**Error Summary**

| | |
|---|---|
| Capitalization | 7 |
| Punctuation: | |
| Apostrophe | 3 |
| Comma | 12 |
| Period | 2 |
| Spelling | 2 |

**THURSDAY**                    **WEEK 2**

Name _____

Despite the length of Cooks expeditions. Very few of his men died from scurvy. Cook was able to prevent scurvy in his men by stocking his ships with sauerkraut. Cook forced his men to eat it daily and he made them eat fresh foods at port stops At first, some sailors didnt want to follow Cooks dietary rules. It wasnt until 1795, sixteen years after Cooks death that lime juice was issued to all british naval vessel. as a result, scurvy began to disappear among british seamen, just as it had with Cooks crews.

**WATCH FOR**

- commas
- names of ethnic groups

| WEDNESDAY | WEEK 2 |
|---|---|

We know today that Vitamin c, or ascorbic acid is neccessary for the formation of tendons ligaments bones and cartilage. Vitamin c is found in lots of fresh foods, including oranges lemons and melons. its also found in tomatos grapefruit and bananas Today, cases of scurvy are rare because it is easy to get fresh food. captain cook didnt know what we do now about vitamins but he made his men follow life-saving directions. with Cooks directions scurvy a deadly disease was prevented

**WATCH FOR**

- commas
- people's names & titles

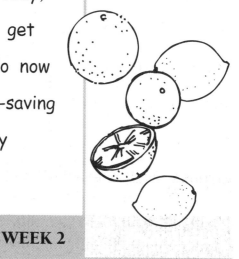

| THURSDAY | WEEK 2 |
|---|---|

Preview the 4 daily lessons to ensure you review or introduce skills that may be unfamiliar to students.

# All Creatures Great and Small

All creatures great and small is a true heartwarming story written by james herriot in this autobiographical tale herriot describes his first year's practicing veterinary medicine. Herriot worked in darrowby england, after he graduated from school in 1937. herriot started as ~~a~~ an assistant to another vet and none of the farmers trusted him at first Funny good and sometimes sad things happened with the farmers and the animals Herriot treated

| Error Summary | |
|---|---|
| Capitalization | 10 |
| Language Usage | 1 |
| Punctuation: | |
|   Comma | 6 |
|   Period | 4 |
|   Other | 1 |
| Spelling | 1 |

**MONDAY**        **WEEK 3**

herriot spent five years in vet school learning all about new procedures and medicines but ~~their~~ there is a great story in All Creatures Great And Small where Herriot doesnt need anything modern at all. A farmer called for help because his prize bull was ill. herriot writes It was a frantic battle for breath, and it looked like a losing one." Herriot took the bulls temperature and it was 110 degrees Fahrenheit. the bull had sunstroke Herriot only needed to spray it with cold water

| Error Summary | |
|---|---|
| Capitalization | 4 |
| Punctuation: | |
|   Apostrophe | 2 |
|   Comma | 3 |
|   Period | 2 |
|   Quotation Mark | 1 |
|   Other | 1 |
| Spelling | 1 |

**TUESDAY**        **WEEK 3**

Name _____

# All Creatures Great and Small

All creatures great and small is a true heartwarming story written by james herriot in this autobiographical tale herriot describes his first year's practicing veterinary medicine. Herriot worked in darrowby england, after he graduated from school in 1937. herriot started as a assistant to another vet and none of the farmers trusted him at first Funny good and sometimes sad things happened with the farmers. and the animals Herriot treated

- commas
- titles of books

| MONDAY | WEEK 3 |

herriot spent five years in vet school learning all about new procedures and medicines but their is a great story in All Creatures Great And Small where Herriot doesnt need anything modern at all. A farmer called for help because his prize bull was ill. herriot writes It was a frantic battle for breath, and it looked like a losing one." Herriot took the bulls temperature and it was 110 degrees Fahrenheit. the bull had sunstroke Herriot only needed to spray it with cold water

- titles of books
- quotes

| TUESDAY | WEEK 3 |

Herriot worked hard, but in all creatures great and small herriot describes farmers who worked even harder. He was called to one farm. Where a milk cow had an infection in her udder. the farmer was young and poor, and he had a wife and small baby. If the milk cow died, it would be a serious loss. after injecting the cow with medicine, herriot told the farmer the only hope was to rub the udder as often as possible. The farmer never slept he rubbed the udder all night, and then he went off to work.

| Error Summary | |
|---|---|
| Capitalization | 10 |
| Language Usage | 1 |
| Punctuation: | |
| Comma | 5 |
| Period | 5 |
| Other | 1 |
| Spelling | 1 |

**WEDNESDAY                                    WEEK 3**

Sometimes when herriot arrived at farms, the animals were not penned up. Herriot arrived at one farm, and the cows he needed to test were out in the pasture. the cows would not come in. A man who could imitate a fly arrived on an old bicycle. When the cows heard the enraged "fly," they ran into the barn. herriot wrote that the man "had a wonderful gift." Perhaps Herriot did not have the gift of imitating a fly, but his book all creatures great and small shows his wonderful gift with words.

| Error Summary | |
|---|---|
| Capitalization | 7 |
| Language Usage | 2 |
| Punctuation: | |
| Comma | 4 |
| Period | 4 |
| Quotation Mark | 1 |
| Other | 1 |
| Spelling | 1 |

**THURSDAY                                      WEEK 3**

Name _____

Herriot worked hard but in all creatures great and small herriot describes farmers who worked even harder. He was called to one farm. Where a milk cow had a infection in her udder. the farmer was young and poor, and he had a wife and small baby. If the milk cow died it would be a serious loss? after injecting the cow with medicine herriot told the farmer the only hope was to rub the udder as often as possable The farmer never slept he rubbed the udder all night and then he went off to work

**WATCH FOR**

- commas
- titles of books

**WEDNESDAY**          **WEEK 3**

Sometimes when herriot arrived at farms the animals were not penned up Herriot arived at one farm and the cows he needs to test were out in the pasture. the cows would not come in? A man who could imitate a fly arrived on a old bicycle When the cows heard the enraged "fly" they ran into the barn. herriot wrote that the man "had a wonderful gift. Perhaps Herriot did not have the gift of imitating a fly but his book all creatures great and small shows his wonderful gift with words

**WATCH FOR**

- special words in quotes
- titles of books

**THURSDAY**          **WEEK 3**

Preview the 4 daily lessons to ensure you review or introduce skills that may be unfamiliar to students.

# John Colter, Explorer

John Colter went with lewis and clark to explore the west When it was time to return, Colter decided to stay colter didnt want to return to the cities where their were busy streets bustling crowds and tall houses. he preferred a house of pine boughs and a roof of stars. Wanting adventure, he stayed and became a "mountain man." he forsook civilization" for the wild country, where only native americans lived

| Error Summary | |
| --- | --- |
| Capitalization | 8 |
| Punctuation: | |
|   Apostrophe | 1 |
|   Comma | 3 |
|   Period | 3 |
|   Quotation Mark | 1 |
| Spelling | 2 |

**MONDAY**                                        **WEEK 4**

---

listening to the call of adventure colter roamed the mountains and the woods. While Colter was hunting beaver in the Rocky mountains in 1807 he heard a strange rumbling sound. suddenly, boiling water began to shoot up from the ground about three and one-half yards away. Higher and higher it rose in a steamy column As hot burning droplets of water began to rain down on Colter's head and shoulder's colter stared in amazement He had just witnessed his first geyser

| Error Summary | |
| --- | --- |
| Capitalization | 5 |
| Punctuation: | |
|   Apostrophe | 1 |
|   Comma | 5 |
|   Period | 3 |
|   Other | 1 |
| Spelling | 1 |

**TUESDAY**                                        **WEEK 4**

Name _____

# John Colter, Explorer

John Colter went with lewis and clark to explore the west When it was time to return. Colter decided to stay colter didnt want to return to the citys where their were busy streets bustling crowds and tall houses. he preferred a house of pine boughs and a roof of stars. Wanting adventure, he stayed and became a "mountain man." he forsook civilization" for the wild country, where only native americans lived

WATCH FOR

- commas
- names of people
- names of places
- names of ethnic groups

**MONDAY**                              **WEEK 4**

listening to the call of adventure colter roamed the mountains and the woods. While Colter was hunting beaver in the Rocky mountains in 1807 he heard a strange rumbling sound. suddenly, boiling water began to shoot up from the ground about three and one half yards away. Higher and higher it rose in a steamy column As hot burning droplets of water began to rain down on Colters head and shoulder's colter stared in amazement He had just witnessed his first geyser

WATCH FOR

- commas
- names of people
- names of places
- hyphens

**TUESDAY**                             **WEEK 4**

after the water stopped boiling out colter did not run away. He carefully ~~careful~~ crept the three and one-half yards to the geyser Gurgling noises still came from the hole and steam wafted above it. Colter was startled because he had never seen anything so strange before. As he continued his journey ~~journie~~ throughout the day colter continued ~~continues~~ to see odd things There were ~~was~~ bubbling puddles of gray and yellow mud and there ~~they're~~ was a crystal pool of scalding blue water. the air had a sulfurous odor, like rotten eggs

**Error Summary**

| | |
|---|---|
| Capitalization | 4 |
| Language Usage | 3 |
| Punctuation: | |
| Comma | 4 |
| Period | 3 |
| Other | 1 |
| Spelling | 2 |

**WEDNESDAY** **WEEK 4**

When colter next met with his friend's he told them about the geysers and other wonders. His friend's laughed at colter because they did not believe him how could there be a land where the ground was hot and boiling water flung itself into the air? Colters friends ~~freinds~~ thought he was telling a tale. they laughed and gave his imaginary land the name Colters Hell. today, we know what colter saw was real and we can see all the wonders he saw, too, if we go to yellowstone national park.

**Error Summary**

| | |
|---|---|
| Capitalization | 9 |
| Punctuation: | |
| Apostrophe | 2 |
| Comma | 2 |
| Period | 1 |
| Other | 1 |
| Spelling | 3 |

**THURSDAY** **WEEK 4**

Name _____

after the water stopped boiling out colter did not run away. He careful crept the three and one half yards to the geyser Gurgling noises still came from the hole and steam wafted above it. Colter was startled because he had never seen anything so strange before. As he continued his journie throughout the day colter continues to see odd things There was bubbling puddles of gray and yellow mud and they're was a crystal pool of scalding blue water. the air had a sulfurous odor, like rotten eggs

- commas
- hyphens

**WEDNESDAY**                                    **WEEK 4**

When colter next met with his friend's he told them about the geysers and other wonders. His friend's laughed at colter because they did not believe him how could there be a land where the ground was hot and boiling water flung itself into the air Colters freinds thought he was telling a tale. they laughed and gave his imaginary land the name Colters Hell. today, we know what colter saw was real and we can see all the wonders he saw, too, if we go to yellowstone national park.

- commas
- names of people
- names of places

**THURSDAY**                                    **WEEK 4**

Preview the 4 daily lessons to ensure you review or introduce skills that may be unfamiliar to students.

# A Letter from Narcissa Whitman

September 29, 1842

dear Jane,

At last, our tiring hard ~~journie~~ journey is over, and we have reached our mission ground in Oregon. we will call our mission "Waiilatpu," for that is what the cayuse Indians call it. This means "the place of the rye grass. ~~Their~~ There is much to do. We must build a home, plow, plant crops, start a school, and hold church services.

**Error Summary**

| | |
|---|---|
| Capitalization | 3 |
| Punctuation: | |
| Comma | 8 |
| Period | 1 |
| Quotation Mark | 2 |
| Spelling | 2 |

**MONDAY**      **WEEK 5**

Now Jane, i am asking if you will come. Are you content to spend the rest of your life on mission ground? We need help for my labor's are great. It is a dreadful ~~journie~~ journey to cross the mountains. You should bring dear, nothing but what you will need for your travels, a sunday suit, and a bible. send the remainder by ship. Jane, if you dont come, please take time to ~~right~~ write.

Your Sister,

Narcissa

**Error Summary**

| | |
|---|---|
| Capitalization | 4 |
| Punctuation: | |
| Apostrophe | 1 |
| Comma | 9 |
| Period | 2 |
| Spelling | 3 |

**TUESDAY**      **WEEK 5**

Name _____

# A Letter from Narcissa Whitman

September 29 1842

- salutations
- special words in quotes
- commas

dear Jane

At last, our tiring hard journie is over and we have reached our mission ground in Oregon we will call our mission Waiilatpu," for that is what the cayuse Indians call it. This means "the place of the rye grass. Their is much to do. We must build a home plow plant crops start a school and hold church services.

| **MONDAY** | **WEEK 5** |
| --- | --- |

Now Jane i am asking if you will come. Are you content to spend the rest of your life on mission ground? We need help for my labor's are great. It is a dreadful journie to cross the mountains. You should bring dear, nothing but what you will need for your travels a sunday suit and a bible send the remainder by ship. Jane if you dont come please take time to right

Your Sister

Narcissa

- closings
- commas

| **TUESDAY** | **WEEK 5** |
| --- | --- |

september 29 1842

dear edward

I am writing you brother to ask you to come join us in our mission work. Edward we need you for there is much to be done. We have only hand tools and our house school and church need to be built. Brother, come and help us turn Waiilatpu our mission into a success did you know our missions name means the place of the rye grass?

| Error Summary | |
| --- | --- |
| Capitalization | 4 |
| Punctuation: | |
|   Apostrophe | 1 |
|   Comma | 11 |
|   Period | 1 |
|   Quotation Mark | 2 |
|   Other | 1 |

**WEDNESDAY**　　　　　　　　　　　**WEEK 5**

You could help plant wheat ~~potatos~~ potatoes and corn while my dear sweet husband marcus takes care of the sick if you come with Jane our sister you two can keep each other company on the long journey. Our desire to be missionaries is strong but ~~their~~ there would be great joy at your arrival. If you dont come Edward please spend time in writing me for i am lonely

    Your Sister

    Narcissa

| Error Summary | |
| --- | --- |
| Capitalization | 4 |
| Punctuation: | |
|   Apostrophe | 1 |
|   Comma | 12 |
|   Period | 2 |
| Spelling | 2 |

**THURSDAY**　　　　　　　　　　　**WEEK 5**

Name _____

september 29 1842

dear edward

    I am writing you brother to ask you to come join us in our mission work. Edward we need you for there is much to be done. We have only hand tools and our house school and church need to be built. Brother, come and help us turn Waiilatpu our mission into a success did you know our missions name means the place of the rye grass.

WATCH FOR

- salutations
- special words in quotes
- commas

---

**WEDNESDAY**                              **WEEK 5**

---

    You could help plant wheat potatos and corn while my dear sweet husband marcus takes care of the sick if you come with Jane our sister you two can keep each other company on the long journey. Our desire to be missionaries is strong but their would be great joy at your arrival. If you dont come Edward please spend time in writing me for i am lonely

    Your Sister

    Narcissa

WATCH FOR

- closings
- commas

---

**THURSDAY**                              **WEEK 5**

Preview the 4 daily lessons to ensure you review or introduce skills that may be unfamiliar to students.

# Terminal Velocity

one right after another nineteen ~~ninteen~~ skydivers jump out of a plane. Although they jump out at different times, they are able to meet in the air and make a circle. By joining hands together, the skydiver's form a human ring high above the ground. How is it possible for them to meet in the air if they all jumped out of the plane at different times? Are some of the skydivers falling faster than the others ~~other~~? Is their ~~there~~ weight affecting how fast they're falling?

| Error Summary | |
| --- | --- |
| Capitalization | 1 |
| Language Usage | 1 |
| Punctuation: | |
|    Comma | 3 |
|    Period | 1 |
|    Other | 3 |
| Spelling | 3 |

**MONDAY**               **WEEK 6**

when an ~~a~~ object is falling through the air, it accelerates as it falls. when something accelerates, its speed increases because it's weight is pulling it downward. There is also a force pushing upward on the object! this upward force is caused by air resistance. air resistance is commonly known as "drag," and the faster an object falls, the greater the drag. it is the combination of acceleration, drag, and something called "terminal velocity" that allows skydivers to control their fall.

| Error Summary | |
| --- | --- |
| Capitalization | 5 |
| Language Usage | 1 |
| Punctuation: | |
|    Apostrophe | 1 |
|    Comma | 4 |
|    Period | 3 |
|    Quotation Mark | 1 |

**TUESDAY**               **WEEK 6**

Name _____

# Terminal Velocity

one right after another ninteen skydivers jump out of a plane. Although they jump out at different times they are able to meet in the air and make a circle. By joining hands together the skydiver's form a human ring high above the ground How is it possible for them to meet in the air if they all jumped out of the plane at different times. Are some of the skydivers falling faster than the other. Is there weight affecting how fast they're falling

**MONDAY**                                    **WEEK 6**

when a object is falling through the air it accelerates as it falls. when something accelerates its speed increases because it's weight is pulling it downward? There is also a force pushing upward on the object! this upward force is caused by air resistance. air resistance is commonly known as "drag," and the faster an object falls, the greater the drag it is the combination of acceleration drag and something called "terminal velocity that allows skydivers to control their fall

**TUESDAY**                                    **WEEK 6**

When the drag pushing upward becomes equal
to the ~~wait~~ weight pulling downward, the skydiver stops
accelerating. the forces on the skydiver have become
balanced, so the skydiver falls at a steady speed.
the skydiver is now at his or her terminal speed,
or Terminal Velocity. Skydiver's cannot change their
weight, but ~~he~~ they can change their drag. if they decrease
their drag, they can fall faster and catch up to their
friends. If they increase ~~they're~~ their drag, on the other
hand, they can decrease their speed.

**WEDNESDAY**  **WEEK 6**

when their arms and legs are spread out,
skydivers ~~normal~~ normally fall at a terminal velocity of about
120 miles per hour. However, if a skydiver turns to
fall head down, his or her drag is lessened drastically.
the skydiver's terminal velocity can increase ~~too~~ to about
180 miles per hour. by moving their arms and legs.
Skydivers change their terminal velocity and control
their fall. In this way, they can catch up to ~~they're~~ their
friends and make a human ring high above the ground.

**THURSDAY**  **WEEK 6**

Name _____

When the drag pushing upward becomes equal to the wait pulling downward the skydiver stops accelerating the forces on the skydiver have become balanced so the skydiver falls at a steady speed! the skydiver is now at his or her terminal speed or Terminal Velocity. Skydiver's cannot change their weight but he can change their drag. if they decrease their drag they can fall faster and catch up to their friends. If they increase they're drag, on the other hand they can decrease their speed?

**WATCH FOR**
- commas

**WEDNESDAY**      **WEEK 6**

when their arms and legs are spread out skydivers normal fall at a terminal velocity of about 120 miles per hour. However if a skydiver turns to fall head down his or her drag is lessened drastically. the skydivers terminal velocity can increase too about 180 miles per hour. by moving their arms and legs. Skydivers change their terminal velocity and control their fall. In this way they can catch up to they're friends and make a human ring high above the ground

**WATCH FOR**
- commas

**THURSDAY**      **WEEK 6**

Preview the 4 daily lessons to ensure you review or introduce skills that may be unfamiliar to students.

# A Petrified Forest

moses harris a mountain man was famous for his tall tails? one of the most experienced guides in the west harris had much to tell about all he had seen done and felt One winter, according to harris he was in the black hills of south dakota he was trapping and hunting and it was very cold snow covered the land He and his horse were tired, hungry, and cold. While searching for food and shelter Harris wandered into a an strange, forgotten valley.

| Error Summary | |
|---|---|
| Capitalization | 12 |
| Language Usage | 1 |
| Punctuation: | |
|    Comma | 11 |
|    Period | 6 |
| Spelling | 2 |

**MONDAY**                                    **WEEK 7**

---

Harris was amazed to see grass that looked thick, green, and fresh green leaves covered the trees, and birds sang songs of spring. Thinking he had found dinner, harris shot at one of the birds. when the bird fell at his feet Harris was astonished to see that the bird was is made of stone Everything, including the grass, trees, and birds, was stone harris brought back a piece peace of hard stone wood to prove his story the wood had become petrified, and it had turned to stone?

| Error Summary | |
|---|---|
| Capitalization | 5 |
| Language Usage | 1 |
| Punctuation: | |
|    Comma | 10 |
|    Period | 5 |
| Spelling | 1 |

**TUESDAY**                                    **WEEK 7**

Name _____

# A Petrified Forest

moses harris a mountain man was famoes for his tall tails? one of the most experienced guides in the west harris had much to tell about all he had seen done and felt One winter, according to harris he was in the black hills of south dakota he was trapping and hunting and it was very cold snow covered the land He and his horse were tired hungry and cold. While searching for food and shelter Harris wandered into an strange forgotten valley

WATCH FOR
- commas
- names of people
- names of places

**MONDAY**                                    **WEEK 7**

---

Harris was amazed to see grass that looked thick green and fresh green leaves covered the trees and birds sang songs of spring. Thinking he had found dinner. harris shot at one of the birds. when the bird fell at his feet Harris was astonished to see that the bird is made of stone Everything including the grass trees and birds was stone harris brought back a peace of hard stone wood to prove his story the wood had become petrified and it had turned to stone?

WATCH FOR
- commas
- names of people

**TUESDAY**                                    **WEEK 7**

The tall tale told by Harris was true in part

because ~~their~~ (there) is such a thing as petrified wood when

something is petrified its turned to stone The stone

wood in fact is a fossil Long ago, trees became

covered by water. Perhaps they ~~fall~~ (fell) into a lake when

a volcano erupted. covered with ash silt and mud

the wood became saturated with water and began to

change It's pores filled in with minerals from the

ash silt and mud covering it. the color of the wood

in fact depends on the minerals that fill in it's pores

| Error Summary | |
|---|---|
| Capitalization | 3 |
| Language Usage | 1 |
| Punctuation: | |
|    Apostrophe | 3 |
|    Comma | 12 |
|    Period | 5 |
| Spelling | 1 |

**WEDNESDAY**           **WEEK 7**

Petrified wood, ~~an~~ (a) type of fossil can be found in

other places besides south dakota ~~Their~~ (There) are petrified

trees measuring 200 feet tall and ten feet wide in

fact in Arizonas petrified forest National park We

can say that people birds or other animals are

petrified but we dont mean they really turned into

stone. we mean that the people birds or other

animals became stiff with fear have you ever been

petrified with fear?

| Error Summary | |
|---|---|
| Capitalization | 7 |
| Language Usage | 1 |
| Punctuation: | |
|    Apostrophe | 2 |
|    Comma | 9 |
|    Period | 3 |
|    Other | 1 |
| Spelling | 1 |

**THURSDAY**           **WEEK 7**

Name _____

The tall tale told by Harris was true in part because their is such a thing as petrified wood when something is petrified its turned to stone The stone wood in fact is a fossil Long ago, trees became covered by water. Perhaps they fall into a lake when a volcano erupted. covered with ash silt and mud the wood became saturated with water and began to change It's pores filled in with minerals from the ash silt and mud covering it. the color of the wood in fact depends on the minerals that fill in it's pores

• commas

**WEDNESDAY**                                    **WEEK 7**

Petrified wood an type of fossil can be found in other places besides south dakota Their are petrified trees measuring 200 feet tall and ten feet wide in fact in Arizonas petrified forest National park We can say that people birds or other animals are petrified but we dont mean they really turned into stone. we mean that the people birds or other animals became stiff with fear have you ever been petrified with fear

• commas
• names of places
• question marks

**THURSDAY**                                    **WEEK 7**

Preview the 4 daily lessons to ensure you review or introduce skills that may be unfamiliar to students.

# Peru's New Museum

Reporter monica vargas describes the new museum [museum] built for one of Perus ancient rulers in her article entitled Peru Devotes Museum to 'Tutankhamen of Americas'. The Lord of Sipan died in the third century and his burial tomb was found in 1987 There was [were] so much gold in sipans tomb that he was called the "Tutankhamen of the Americas" Tutankhamen was an [a] ancient egyptian ruler known for his gold tomb.

| **Error Summary** | |
|---|---|
| Capitalization | 4 |
| Language Usage | 2 |
| Punctuation: | |
| Apostrophe | 2 |
| Comma | 1 |
| Period | 3 |
| Quotation Mark | 3 |
| Spelling | 1 |

**MONDAY**      **WEEK 8**

an archaeologist walter alva discovered Sipans tomb Alva began [begin] to dig when he heard rumors about people stealing treasure "gangs were destroying these monuments" Alva is quoted as saying in the article Peru Devotes Museum to 'Tutankhamen of Americas.' armed police guarded the tomb 24 hours a day while Alva worked [works]. alva found gold ornaments and armor He also found Sipans wife, three servants, guards, and even Sipan's dog.

| **Error Summary** | |
|---|---|
| Capitalization | 6 |
| Language Usage | 2 |
| Punctuation: | |
| Apostrophe | 2 |
| Comma | 7 |
| Period | 4 |
| Quotation Mark | 2 |

**TUESDAY**      **WEEK 8**

Name _____

# Peru's New Museum

Reporter monica vargas describes the new museam built for one of Perus ancient rulers in her article entitled Peru Devotes Museum to 'Tutankhamen of Americas'. The Lord of Sipan died in the third century and his burial tomb was found in 1987 There were so much gold in sipans tomb that he was called the Tutankhamen of the Americas" Tutankhamen was a ancient egyptian ruler known for his gold tomb

• titles of articles
• special words in quotes

**MONDAY**                                        **WEEK 8**

---

an archaeologist walter alva discovered Sipans tomb Alva begin to dig when he heard rumors about people stealing treasure "gangs were destroying these monuments" Alva is quoted as saying in the article Peru Devotes Museum to 'Tutankhamen of Americas.' armed police guarded the tomb 24 hours a day while Alva works. alva found gold ornaments and armor He also found Sipans wife three servants guards and even Sipan's dog

• titles of articles
• quotes

**TUESDAY**                                       **WEEK 8**

Peru̱s new M̲useum shows more than Sipan̲s gold ornaments. "i̲t's a museum-mausoleum that will show how he was buried Alva ~~a~~ an archaeologist explained. s̲ipan was a Moche ruler and the moches ~~rules~~ ruled the p̲acific coast from the F̲irst to the S̲ixth ~~centurys~~ centuries. t̲he new museum is shaped like a Moche pyramid. Constructed from fiberglass bricks the museum resembles the original burial ~~cite~~ site. t̲o protect its 1,500 precious pieces, the museum doesn̲t have ~~no~~ any windows.

| Error Summary | |
| --- | --- |
| Capitalization | 10 |
| Language Usage | 3 |
| Punctuation: | |
| Apostrophe | 3 |
| Comma | 5 |
| Period | 1 |
| Quotation Mark | 1 |
| Spelling | 2 |

**WEDNESDAY**　　　　　**WEEK 8**

Vargas reports in her article, "Peru Devotes Museum to 'Tutankhamen of Americas'," that some of the ~~peaces~~ pieces in the ~~musoam~~ museum were recovered from grave robbers. A special law in the u̲nited s̲tates makes it illegal to sell Sipan̲s treasures and the Federal b̲ureau of i̲nvestigation ~~help~~ helped recover some pieces valued at over $1.6 million. "This is the biggest museum dedicated to a single find archaeologist Alva said. The museum receives up to 1,000 ~~visitor~~ visitors a day.

| Error Summary | |
| --- | --- |
| Capitalization | 4 |
| Language Usage | 2 |
| Punctuation: | |
| Apostrophe | 1 |
| Comma | 2 |
| Period | 1 |
| Quotation Mark | 4 |
| Spelling | 2 |

**THURSDAY**　　　　　**WEEK 8**

Name _____

Perus new Museum shows more than Sipans gold ornaments. "it's a museum-mausoleum that will show how he was buried Alva a archaeologist explained. sipan was a Moche ruler and the moches rules the pacific coast from the First to the Sixth centurys. the new museum is shaped like a Moche pyramid. Constructed from fiberglass bricks the museum resembles the original burial cite. to protect its 1,500 precious pieces, the museum doesnt have no windows

**WATCH FOR**

- quotes
- names of ethnic groups

| **WEDNESDAY** | **WEEK 8** |

Vargas reports in her article, Peru Devotes Museum to 'Tutankhamen of Americas', that some of the peaces in the museam were recovered from grave robbers. A special law in the united states makes it illegal to sell Sipans treasures and the Federal bureau of investigation help recover some pieces valued at over $1.6 million. This is the biggest museum dedicated to a single find archaeologist Alva said. The museum receives up to 1,000 visitor a day

**WATCH FOR**

- titles of articles

| **THURSDAY** | **WEEK 8** |

Preview the 4 daily lessons to ensure you review or introduce skills that may be unfamiliar to students.

# A Change of Plans

to make his tires last longer thirteen-year-old
eduardo pushed his bike along the gravel path. it was
an old bike but it was new for Eduardo he had bought
him with the money he had earned weeding hoeing
and working during spring vacation he used the bike
to make the three-mile trip from the farm where his
parents were working to school. he hummed the song
"take me out to The Ballgame as he walked

| Error Summary | |
|---|---|
| Capitalization | 10 |
| Language Usage | 2 |
| Punctuation: | |
| Comma | 4 |
| Period | 3 |
| Quotation Mark | 1 |
| Other | 2 |

**MONDAY**                                          **WEEK 9**

---

eduardo knew he would have to work that summer
but now he was playing baseball on the school team.
With his bike he didnt have to worry about catching
the school bus for the three-mile ride back to the
farm he had been at the same school for three
months now and he was finally catching up on Reading
Math and science While his parents worked at the
farm Eduardo helped his brothers carlos and juan with
schoolwork, chores and dinner preparations

| Error Summary | |
|---|---|
| Capitalization | 6 |
| Language Usage | 1 |
| Punctuation: | |
| Apostrophe | 1 |
| Comma | 9 |
| Period | 3 |
| Other | 1 |
| Spelling | 2 |

**TUESDAY**                                          **WEEK 9**

Name _____

# A Change of Plans

to make his tires last longer thirteen-year old eduardo pushed his bike along the gravel path. it was a old bike but it was new for Eduardo he had bought him with the money he had earned weeding hoeing and working during spring vacation he used the bike to make the three mile trip from the farm where his parents were working to school. he hummed the song "take me out to The Ballgame as he walked

- hyphens
- song titles
- commas

| | |
|---|---|
| **MONDAY** | **WEEK 9** |

eduardo knew he wood have to work that summer but now he was playing baseball on the school team. With his bike we didnt have to worry about catching the school bus for the three mile ride back to the farm he had been at the same school for three months now and he was finally catching up on Reading Math and sceince While his parents worked at the farm Eduardo helped his brothers carlos and juan with schoolwork, chores and dinner preparations

- hyphens
- commas

| | |
|---|---|
| **TUESDAY** | **WEEK 9** |

when eduardo came to the end of his three-mile journey back to the farm he was surprised to find his ~~her~~ Father Mother and brothers loading up ~~there~~ their van They were moving to a different farm Uncle alberto his father's brother had found them a new farm to work on they would ~~urn~~ earn more money and have a better house but they needed to start work right away Now, even though eduardo had been practicing with the schools baseball team He wouldnt be able to play in any of their games

**WEDNESDAY                                        WEEK 9**

| Error Summary | |
|---|---|
| Capitalization | 8 |
| Language Usage | 1 |
| Punctuation: | |
| Apostrophe | 3 |
| Comma | 7 |
| Period | 5 |
| Other | 1 |
| Spelling | 2 |

eduardo took his books to his eleven-year-old neighbor, Roberto, and ~~axed~~ asked him to return them to the school. not wanting anyone to think he didnt like baseball. Eduardo wrote a good-bye note to ~~her~~ his teacher The note explained about the move He wrote, I hope the team wins. as the van started down the road eduardo laughed at the off-key singing of his Father Mother and brothers. They sang Take Me out to the ballgame. Today, Eduardo ~~wood~~ would listen, but he knew he would someday play baseball again

**THURSDAY                                         WEEK 9**

| Error Summary | |
|---|---|
| Capitalization | 8 |
| Language Usage | 1 |
| Punctuation: | |
| Apostrophe | 1 |
| Comma | 8 |
| Period | 3 |
| Quotation Mark | 4 |
| Other | 4 |
| Spelling | 2 |

Name _____

when eduardo came to the end of his three mile journey back to the farm he was surprised to find her Father Mother and brothers loading up there van They were moving to a different farm Uncle alberto his fathers brother had found them a new farm to work on they would urn more money and have a better house but they needed to start work right away? Now, even though eduardo had been practicing with the schools baseball team. He wouldnt be able to play in any of their games

WATCH FOR

• hyphens
• commas

| WEDNESDAY | WEEK 9 |

eduardo took his books to his eleven year old neighbor Roberto and axed him to return them to the school. not wanting anyone to think he didnt like baseball. Eduardo wrote a good bye note to her teacher? The note explained about the move He wrote I hope the team wins. as the van started down the road eduardo laughed at the off key singing of his Father Mother and brothers. They sang Take Me out to the ballgame. Today, Eduardo wood listen but he knew he would someday play baseball again

WATCH FOR

• hyphens
• song titles
• commas

| THURSDAY | WEEK 9 |

Preview the 4 daily lessons to ensure you review or introduce skills that may be unfamiliar to students.

# Greenland Letters

august 5, 2002

dear robert T wells

I've never had a pen pal before, but then i bet youve never been to greenland. Greenland, the worlds largest island, is mostly covered by ~~a~~ an ice cap. in the center of this island, believe it or not, the ice cap measures ~~mesures~~ 9,800 Ft. deep! Did you know that thousand's of icebergs are formed each year in Greenland?

### Error Summary

| | |
|---|---|
| Capitalization | 8 |
| Language Usage | 1 |
| Punctuation: | |
| Apostrophe | 3 |
| Comma | 7 |
| Period | 3 |
| Other | 1 |
| Spelling | 2 |

**MONDAY**                                    **WEEK 10**

greenlands capital, Nuuk, is on the southwestern coast. back in the tenth century, eric the red explored greenland. Eric the red, incredible as it may seem, was the father of leif eriksson.

Greenland exports hides, fish, and fish oil, and our biggest trading partner is denmark. Ill tell you more after you write ~~rite~~ back.

your new friend and Pen Pal,

eric s. knudsen.

### Error Summary

| | |
|---|---|
| Capitalization | 15 |
| Punctuation: | |
| Apostrophe | 2 |
| Comma | 8 |
| Period | 4 |
| Spelling | 1 |

**TUESDAY**                                    **WEEK 10**

Name

# Greenland Letters

august 5 2002

WATCH FOR

• salutations

• interruptions

• question marks

dear robert T wells

Ive never had a pen pal before but then i bet youve never been to greenland Greenland the worlds largest island is mostly covered by a ice cap. in the center of this island believe it or not the ice cap mesures 9,800 Ft deep! Did you know that thousand's of icebergs are formed each year in Greenland.

Dear Robert,

Your Friend,
Eric

**MONDAY**                                                    **WEEK 10**

greenlands capital, Nuuk is on the southwestern coast. back in the tenth century eric the red explored greenland. Eric the red incredible as it may seem was the father of leif eriksson

Greenland exports hides fish and fish oil and our biggest trading partner is denmark. Ill tell you more after you rite back

your new friend and Pen Pal.

eric s knudsen.

WATCH FOR

• closings

• interruptions

**TUESDAY**                                                    **WEEK 10**

december 21, 2002

dear Robert T. Wells

Did you know that mammals live in greenland? besides polar bears we have wolves, lemmings, reindeer and, of course, whales and seals. There are lots of seabirds. But they're not mammals.

it is dark now, but the long days of summer will make up for the lack of light now. you mentioned the trips you took on memorial day and presidents' day. could you tell me more about those holidays and how you celebrate them?

**Error Summary**

| | |
|---|---|
| Capitalization | 12 |
| Punctuation: | |
|   Comma | 9 |
|   Period | 2 |
|   Other | 2 |
| Spelling | 2 |

**WEDNESDAY**　　　　　　　　　　**WEEK 10**

if you want to be a meteorologist, you should come here. Greenland is the source of many of the weather changes in the northern hemisphere. Brigette, my sister, is studying to be a meteorologist.

Do you really eat Turkey on thanksgiving? What do you eat on new year's day?

Did you know that greenland is internally self-governing, but it's actually part of the kingdom of denmark? Isn't that similar to puerto rico?

sincerely,

eric s. knudsen

**Error Summary**

| | |
|---|---|
| Capitalization | 15 |
| Punctuation: | |
|   Apostrophe | 2 |
|   Comma | 5 |
|   Period | 3 |
|   Other | 5 |
| Spelling | 3 |

**THURSDAY**　　　　　　　　　　**WEEK 10**

Name —————————————————————————

december 21 2002

dear Robert T Wells

Did you know that mammals live in greenland. besides polar bears we have wolves lemmings reindeer and, of course whales and seals. Their are lots of seabirds But their not mammals.

it is dark now but the long days of summer will make up for the lack of light now. you mentioned the trips you took on memorial day and presidents' day could you tell me more about those holidays and how you celebrate them

WATCH FOR
- salutations
- commas
- question marks

| WEDNESDAY | WEEK 10 |
|---|---|

if you want to be a meteorologist you should come here Greenland is the source of many of the whether changes in the northern hemisphere. Brigette my sister is studing to be a meteorologist

Do you really eat Turkey on thanksgiving. What do you eat on new year's day

Did you no that greenland is internally self governing but its actually part of the kingdom of denmark Isnt that similar to puerto rico

sincerely

eric s knudsen

WATCH FOR
- closings
- question marks
- hyphens

Dear Robert,

Your Friend,
Eric

| THURSDAY | WEEK 10 |
|---|---|

Preview the 4 daily lessons to ensure you review or introduce skills that may be unfamiliar to students.

# City of Mystery

about 30 miles northeast of mexico city mexico, are the ruins of a great city Archaeologists, or "Detectives of the Past" are working to dig up facts about this city of mystery. by digging and studying archaeologists know that there ~~are~~ were small villages in the area around 100 BC. Just 300 years later there were 75,000 people living in the city Twice as many people lived ~~their~~ there by AD 600 and it had grown into one of the largest ~~citys~~ cities in the world

**MONDAY**     **WEEK 11**

**Error Summary**

| Capitalization | 7 |
|---|---|
| Language Usage | 1 |
| Punctuation: | |
|   Comma | 6 |
|   Period | 6 |
|   Quotation Mark | 1 |
| Spelling | 2 |

the aztecs settled in this area hundreds of years after the ancient city had been destroyed They found empty buildings, masks and tools of stone, pottery, and two large pyramids. The larger pyramid was as tall as a 20-story building, and it's base covered 500,000 square feet. when they walked ~~threw~~ through the ruins, the aztecs couldnt ~~beleive~~ believe that men had built the city. they named the place the City of the Gods, And they used the city ruins as a place to pray

**TUESDAY**     **WEEK 11**

**Error Summary**

| Capitalization | 6 |
|---|---|
| Punctuation: | |
|   Apostrophe | 2 |
|   Comma | 5 |
|   Period | 2 |
| Spelling | 2 |

Name _____

# City of Mystery

- special words in quotes
- abbreviations

about 30 miles northeast of mexico city mexico, are the ruins of a great city Archaeologists or Detectives of the Past" are working to dig up facts about this city of mystery. by digging and studying archaeologists know that there are small villages in the area around 100 BC. Just 300 years later there were 75,000 people living in the city Twice as many people lived their by AD 600 and it had grown into one of the largest citys in the world

| MONDAY | WEEK 11 |
|---|---|

- commas

the aztecs settled in this area hundreds of years after the ancient city had been destroyed They found empty buildings masks and tools of stone, pottery and two large pyramids. The larger pyramid was as tall as a 20-story building and it's base covered 500,000 square feet. when they walked threw the ruins the aztecs couldnt beleive that men had built the city. they named the place the City of the Gods. And they used the city ruins as a place to pray

| TUESDAY | WEEK 11 |
|---|---|

we can tell from the ruins that the city
studied
builders ~~studyed~~ the stars, planets, and geometry.
were
Their buildings, for example, ~~was~~ built so the walls
their
faced North, South, west and east and ~~there~~ streets
were planned using the position of the solar system.
Apartment complexes able to hold 60 to 100 people
were built around a patio. by looking at the artifacts
in the apartments, we can tell that people came from
all over mexico to live in this city. They may have
come because of the citys big marketplace.

**Error Summary**

| | |
|---|---|
| Capitalization | 5 |
| Language Usage | 1 |
| Punctuation: | |
| Apostrophe | 1 |
| Comma | 9 |
| Period | 3 |
| Spelling | 2 |

**WEDNESDAY**　　　**WEEK 11**

pots, masks, salt, fish, and earrings carved from
were
jade ~~was~~ probably traded at the city market. There
knives
wasn't anything made of metal, but ~~knifes~~, tools, and
mirrors made of obsidian, a type of stone, were
traded. Big wall paintings, or murals, have been found
in buildings and underground rooms. Markings on the
paintings show that the people probably used a form
There
of picture writing. ~~Their~~ is still much to know about
this city of mystery, as the past is dug up, new things
are
~~is~~ learned.

**Error Summary**

| | |
|---|---|
| Capitalization | 2 |
| Language Usage | 2 |
| Punctuation: | |
| Comma | 11 |
| Period | 5 |
| Spelling | 2 |

**THURSDAY**　　　**WEEK 11**

Name _____

we can tell from the ruins that the city builders studied the stars planets and geometry. Their buildings for example was built so the walls faced North South west and east and there streets were planned using the position of the solar system Apartment complexes able to hold 60 to 100 people were built around a patio. by looking at the artifacts in the apartments we can tell that people came from all over mexico to live in this city They may have come because of the citys big marketplace

**WEDNESDAY**                                    **WEEK 11**

pots masks salt fish and earrings carved from jade was probably traded at the city market There wasn't anything made of metal but knifes tools and mirrors made of obsidian a type of stone were traded. Big wall paintings or murals, have been found in buildings and underground rooms Markings on the paintings show that the people probably used a form of picture writing Their is still much to know about this city of mystery as the past is dug up new things is learned

**THURSDAY**                                    **WEEK 11**

Preview the 4 daily lessons to ensure you review or introduce skills that may be unfamiliar to students.

# Pandora's Mysterious Box

When Pandora was created by the gods and goddesses of mount olympus each one gave her a special gift they blessed her with beauty wisdom and happiness
happyness. When they had finished bestowing their gifts? The gods agreed that he was almost perfect.

"Wait a goddess said. There is another gift she must have. If she has no interest in learning about all on earth Pandora will be bored." The goddess therefore also gave her curiosity.

| Error Summary | |
|---|---|
| Capitalization | 5 |
| Language Usage | 1 |
| Punctuation: | |
|   Comma | 8 |
|   Period | 1 |
|   Quotation Mark | 2 |
| Spelling | 2 |

**MONDAY**        **WEEK 12**

Before pandora left the house of the god's she was given a chest that was tyed and locked jupiter cautioned her, What ever happens, do not open the chest. Keep it locked forever? The contents will bring great unhappiness to the world.

On Earth, pandora was loved and admired by everyone her laughter and song charmed the birds and animals in the forests. She chose a handsome partner epimetheus as her Husband. They lived a happy friends
life dancing singing and celebrating with their freinds.

| Error Summary | |
|---|---|
| Capitalization | 6 |
| Punctuation: | |
|   Comma | 5 |
|   Period | 4 |
|   Quotation Mark | 2 |
| Spelling | 4 |

**TUESDAY**        **WEEK 12**

Name —————————————————

# Pandora's Mysterious Box

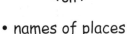

When Pandora was created by the gods and goddesses of mount olympus each one gave her a special gift they blessed her with beauty wisdom and happyness. When they had finished be stowing their gifts? The gods agreed that he was almost perfect.

"Wait a goddess said. There is another gift she must have. If she has no interest in learning about all on earth Pandora will be bored." The goddess therefore also gave her curiosity.

• names of places
• dialog

**MONDAY**                              **WEEK 12**

Before pandora left the house of the god's she was given a chest that was tyed and locked jupiter cautioned her, What ever happens, do not open the chest. Keep it locked forever? The contents will bring great unhappiness to the world.

On Earth, pandora was loved and admired by everyone her laughter and song charmed the birds and animals in the forests. She chose a handsome partner epimetheus as her Husband. They lived a happy life dancing singing and celebrating with their freinds

• names of people
• dialog

**TUESDAY**                              **WEEK 12**

For a long time, the chest sat undisturbed in a corner of Pandora's house when visitors came to call, they commented on the beautiful carvings. That decorated the lid. Many asked to look inside the chest, but pandora explained that it was a gift from the gods that was never to be opened. unfortunately, that only prompted an even greater interest in some of the visitors.

"A gift from the gods?" asked one. "Then, of course, it must hold great magic or priceless jewels. no chest should be closed for ever."

| Error Summary | |
| --- | --- |
| Capitalization | 5 |
| Language Usage | 2 |
| Punctuation: | |
| Apostrophe | 1 |
| Comma | 5 |
| Period | 3 |
| Quotation Mark | 3 |
| Spelling | 2 |

**WEDNESDAY**                                    **WEEK 12**

"One quick look inside this beautiful gift from the gods would surely do no harm," insisted another visitor. "No one would ever need to know. Even the god's themselves would not learn of it."

No matter how much her guests pleaded, pandora refused to follow their suggestions that she disobey Jupiter's instructions. As time went by, however, curiosity about the contents of the mysterious chest began to take hold of pandora. Pandora soon found herself wondering about the chest morning, noon, and night.

| Error Summary | |
| --- | --- |
| Capitalization | 2 |
| Language Usage | 1 |
| Punctuation: | |
| Apostrophe | 1 |
| Comma | 5 |
| Period | 1 |
| Quotation Mark | 2 |
| Spelling | 4 |

**THURSDAY**                                    **WEEK 12**

Name _____

For a long time the chest sat undisturbed in a corner of Pandoras house when visitors came to call they comented on the beautiful carvings. That decorated the lid. Many asked to look inside the chest but pandora explained that they was a gift from the gods that was never to be opened unfortunately, that only prompt an even greater interest in some of the visitors.

"A gift from the gods? asked one. Then of course it must hold great magic or priceless jewels. no chest should be closed for ever.

• dialog

**WEDNESDAY                    WEEK 12**

One quick look inside this beautiful gift from the gods would sureley do no harm, insisted another visitor. "No one would ever need to know. Even the god's them selves would not learn of it."

No matter how much her guests pleaded pandora refused to follow their suggestions that he disobey Jupiters instructions. As time went by however curiosity about the contents of the mysterious chest began to take hold of pandora. Pandora soon found herself wondering about the chest mourning noon and night

• dialog

**THURSDAY                    WEEK 12**

Preview the 4 daily lessons to ensure you review or introduce skills that may be unfamiliar to students.

# Where in the World?

Were off on a mystery vacation to a very narrow country Be sure to pack skis snow gear a swimsuit beach towel and hat be ready to see some fascinating birds, including Penguins Flamingoes and if we're lucky an andean condor. Well need to take a ship and travel far across a ocean to see all of this country but on the mainland we have our choice between belching volcanoes arid deserts and snowy mountains

(correction: *an* across *a* ocean; *volcanoes* above volcanos; *deserts* above desserts)

| Error Summary | |
|---|---|
| Capitalization | 4 |
| Language Usage | 1 |
| Punctuation: | |
| Apostrophe | 2 |
| Comma | 10 |
| Period | 3 |
| Spelling | 2 |

**MONDAY**　　　　　**WEEK 13**

---

Our trip will begin at 900 am when our boat docks in the sunny town of arica The pacific ocean currents keep the temperature in Arica about the same all year so whether its winter or summer we can enjoy swimming and playing at the beach. just a few hours away from the western border is the eastern border. in the high eastern mountains we can ski or we can visit lago chungará, one of the highest lakes in the world. as we travel south well see herds of vicuña and flocks of ñandú

(corrections: *whether* above wether; *highest* above higher)

| Error Summary | |
|---|---|
| Capitalization | 8 |
| Language Usage | 1 |
| Punctuation: | |
| Apostrophe | 2 |
| Comma | 5 |
| Period | 4 |
| Other | 1 |
| Spelling | 1 |

**TUESDAY**　　　　　**WEEK 13**

Name _____

# Where in the World?

Were off on a mystery vacation to a very narrow country Be sure to pack skis snow gear a swimsuit beach towel and hat be ready to see some fascinating birds, including Penguins Flamingoes and if we're lucky an andean condor. Well need to take a ship and travel far across a ocean to see all of this country but on the mainland we have our choice between belching volcanos arid desserts and snowy mountains

WATCH FOR

- commas

**MONDAY**                                        **WEEK 13**

Our trip will begin at 900 am when our boat docks in the sunny town of arica? The pacific ocean currents keep the temperature in Arica about the same all year so wether its winter or summer we can enjoy swimming and playing at the beach. just a few hours away from the western border is the eastern border. in the high eastern mountains we can ski or we can visit lago chungará, one of the higher lakes in the world. as we travel south well see herds of vicuña and flocks of ñandú

WATCH FOR

- time
- abbreviations
- names of places

**TUESDAY**                                        **WEEK 13**

In santiago the capital city we will tour some of the old spanish-style churches and building. before heading down to the strait of Magellan they will take a long ocean voyage to easter island. Our boat will leave at 100 pm we will want to take pictures of the giant stone statues that dot this tiny speck of land. the statues believe it or not are 5.5 to 7 meters (18 to 22 ft) tall they we're carved with simple hand tools. How they were moved too where they stand today is a real mystery?

**Error Summary**

| | |
|---|---|
| Capitalization | 9 |
| Language Usage | 2 |
| Punctuation: | |
| Comma | 5 |
| Period | 5 |
| Other | 2 |
| Spelling | 3 |

**WEDNESDAY**                    **WEEK 13**

Our schedule says that she will return from easter Island at 330 P.M. Even if the boat docks late we will still have time to relax before heading up to the mountains for some river-rafting adventures. our final destination will be to another continent from punta arenas on the strait of magellan we will catch a cruise ship. it leaves at 545 am. but its worth it to get up so early. It is going to take us to a penguin rookery on the continent of antarctica

**Error Summary**

| | |
|---|---|
| Capitalization | 11 |
| Language Usage | 1 |
| Punctuation: | |
| Apostrophe | 1 |
| Comma | 2 |
| Period | 4 |
| Other | 3 |

**THURSDAY**                    **WEEK 13**

Name _____

In santiago the capital city we will tour some of the old spanish style churchs and building. before heading down to the strait of Magellan they will take a long ocean voyage to easter island. Our boat will leave at 100 pm we will want to take pictures of the giant stone statues that dot this tiny speck of land. the statues believe it or not are 5.5 to 7 meters (18 to 22 ft) tall they we're carved with simple hand tools. How they were moved too where they stand today is a real mystery?

- time
- abbreviations
- hyphens

**WEDNESDAY**                                    **WEEK 13**

Our schedule says that she will return from easter Island at 330 P.M. Even if the boat docks late we will still have time to relax before heading up to the mountains for some river rafting adventures. our final destination will be to another continent from punta arenas on the strait of magellan we will catch a cruise ship. it leaves at 545 am, but its worth it to get up so early. It is going to take us to a penguin rookery on the continent of antarctica

- time
- abbreviations
- hyphens

**THURSDAY**                                    **WEEK 13**

Preview the 4 daily lessons to ensure you review or introduce skills that may be unfamiliar to students.

# Sir Ernest Shackleton

sir ernest shackleton was ~~a~~ an explorer but he was an amazing leader above all else. he felt great responsibility for all of his men and He wouldnt ask them to do anything that he wouldnt do himself? Shackleton an optimist had big dreams. He ~~planed~~ planned to lead ~~a~~ an expedition 1,800 miles across antarctica. On august, 8 1914 Shackleton ~~sets~~ set sail in his ship Endurance. he had no idea of the ~~tradgedy~~ tragedy that was going to befall him?

**Error Summary**

| | |
|---|---|
| Capitalization | 8 |
| Language Usage | 3 |
| Punctuation: | |
| Apostrophe | 2 |
| Comma | 6 |
| Period | 2 |
| Other | 1 |
| Spelling | 2 |

**MONDAY                    WEEK 14**

On january 18 1915 the endurance became frozen in the pack ice at the southern edge of the weddell sea. the ship ~~drift~~ drifted powerless and frozen solid for nine months. On october 27, the unthinkable happened. Crushed by ice, the endurance began to sink and it had to be abandoned. the men we're alone. Underneath ~~there~~ their feet lay 12,000 feet of deep cold Ocean? shackleton didnt allow his men to ~~beleive~~ believe that they would perish. So now well go home" shackleton told them

**Error Summary**

| | |
|---|---|
| Capitalization | 11 |
| Language Usage | 1 |
| Punctuation: | |
| Apostrophe | 2 |
| Comma | 5 |
| Period | 2 |
| Quotation Mark | 1 |
| Other | 2 |
| Spelling | 3 |

**TUESDAY                   WEEK 14**

Name _____

# Sir Ernest Shackleton

sir ernest shackleton was a explorer but he was an amazing leader above all else. he felt great responsibility for all of his men and He wouldnt ask them to do anything that he wouldnt do himself? Shackleton an optimist had big dreams. He planed to lead a expedition 1,800 miles across antarctica. On august, 8. 1914 Shackleton sets sail in his ship Endurance. he had no idea of the tradgedy that was going to befall him?

• names of ships
• commas

**MONDAY**                                    **WEEK 14**

On january 18 1915 the endurance became frozen in the pack ice at the southern edge of the weddell sea. the ship drift powerless and frozen solid for nine months. On october 27, the unthinkable happened. Crushed by ice, the endurance began to sink and it had to be abandoned. the men we're alone. Underneath there feet lay 12,000 feet of deep cold Ocean? shackleton didnt allow his men to beleive that they would perish. So now well go home" shackleton told them

• names of ships
• commas
• quotes

**TUESDAY**                                    **WEEK 14**

the men floated on ice floes until april 9, 1916. they ate penguins, seals, and the last of their ~~supplys~~ supplies. When one man spilled his cup of precious milk, shackleton silently poured some of his own into the mans cup. Other men ~~follows~~ followed Shackletons' lead. One night, the floe cracked in two and a man fell into the crack. Shackleton, ever alert, pulled the man out seconds before the floe smashed back together. shackleton worried, but he never let his men know. he wouldnt let any one give up hope.

| Error Summary | |
| --- | --- |
| Capitalization | 6 |
| Language Usage | 1 |
| Punctuation: | |
| Apostrophe | 3 |
| Comma | 6 |
| Period | 1 |
| Spelling | 2 |

**WEDNESDAY**　　　　**WEEK 14**

At the edge of the ice pack, the men launched ~~there~~ their lifeboats. for six long days, they rowed in the tiny open boats. Wet, sick, and covered with sores, They landed on ~~a~~ an uninhabited island. help was over 800 miles away across one of the worlds most dangerous oceans? Most men would have given up, but shackleton did not. He ~~sail~~ sailed with five men, leaving 22 behind. Looking death in the eye, he refused to ~~quite.~~ quit. He made it to land, and he eventually rescued his men. His men never gave up hope, they knew their leader would return.

| Error Summary | |
| --- | --- |
| Capitalization | 5 |
| Language Usage | 2 |
| Punctuation: | |
| Apostrophe | 1 |
| Comma | 7 |
| Period | 3 |
| Spelling | 2 |

**THURSDAY**　　　　**WEEK 14**

Name _____

the men floated on ice floes until april 9 1916. they ate penguins seals and the last of their supplys. When one man spilled his cup of precious milk shackleton silently poured some of his own into the mans cup. Other men follows Shackletons' lead. One night, the floe cracked in two and a man fell into the crack. Shackleton ever alert pulled the man out seconds before the floe smashed back together. shackleton worried, but he never let his men know. he wouldnt let any one give up hope

WATCH FOR

• commas

**WEDNESDAY**                                          **WEEK 14**

At the edge of the ice pack the men launched there lifeboats. for six long days, they rowed in the tiny open boats. Wet sick and covered with sores. They landed on a uninhabited island. help was over 800 miles away across one of the worlds most dangerous oceans? Most men would have given up but shackleton did not. He sail with five men, leaving 22 behind. Looking death in the eye he refused to quite. He made it to land and he eventually rescued his men. His men never gave up hope they knew their leader would return

WATCH FOR

• commas

**THURSDAY**                                          **WEEK 14**

Preview the 4 daily lessons to ensure you review or introduce skills that may be unfamiliar to students.

# Schools Need Principles

walk into most schools these days and you are sure to find soda and candy machines Some principals parents and health workers are concerned because they say that students ~~is~~ (are) being encouraged to eat poorly Instead of buying a school lunch or milk for example a student may buy a soda candy bar and chips? people ~~whom~~ (who) support these machines in school Point out that no one has to use them. everyone has ~~an~~ (a) choice

| Error Summary | |
|---|---|
| Capitalization | 4 |
| Language Usage | 3 |
| Punctuation: | |
| Comma | 7 |
| Period | 5 |

**MONDAY**                                      **WEEK 15**

while I agree that everyone has a choice i believe that ~~their~~ (there) isnt any reason for a school to encourage poor eating habits What example do we show our students when ~~I~~ (we) say "eat well" and then offer them junk food? Principals teachers and students need to take action because the poor physical fitness of americans has become a national problem. the truth is in fact that the issue is money schools ~~is payed~~ (are paid) to allow vending machines onsite and they are also paid ~~an~~ (a) percentage of the amount sold

| Error Summary | |
|---|---|
| Capitalization | 6 |
| Language Usage | 3 |
| Punctuation: | |
| Apostrophe | 1 |
| Comma | 8 |
| Period | 3 |
| Other | 1 |
| Spelling | 2 |

**TUESDAY**                                     **WEEK 15**

Name _____

# Schools Need Principles

walk into most schools these days and you are sure to find soda and candy machines Some principals parents and health workers are concerned because they say that students is being encouraged to eat poorly Instead of buying a school lunch or milk for example a student may buy a soda candy bar and chips? people whom support these machines in school. Point out that no one has to use them. everyone has an choice

while I agree that everyone has a choice i believe that their isnt any reason for a school to encourage poor eating habits What example do we show our students when I say "eat well" and then offer them junk food Principals teachers and students need to take action because the poor physical fitness of americans has become a national problem. the truth is in fact that the issue is money? schools is payed to allow vending machines onsite and they are also paid an percentage of the amount sold

WATCH FOR

• quotes

the teachers principles and adults who allow soda and candy machines point out that the money earned is used to improve the schools. by allowing the machines schools can pay for extra programs? Students will buy junk food anyway" they say. "they should buy it from us because we will use the money on the school" that logic i believe sends the wrong message to the students. That message to the students is "Money is the most important thing in the world.

| Error Summary | |
| --- | --- |
| Capitalization | 6 |
| Language Usage | 2 |
| Punctuation: | |
| Comma | 6 |
| Period | 3 |
| Quotation Mark | 2 |
| Spelling | 3 |

**WEDNESDAY**　　　　　　　　　　　**WEEK 15**

While its true that money is necessary for a school to run principals school districts and others cant depend on soda and vending machines. Their presence says to the students "don't pay attention to what we teach you about nutrition give us money! The solution i believe is a compromise Soda and vending machines may be allowed but they should be available only at certain times. other machines however should offer milk fresh fruit and other healthy foods?

| Error Summary | |
| --- | --- |
| Capitalization | 4 |
| Language Usage | 1 |
| Punctuation: | |
| Apostrophe | 2 |
| Comma | 11 |
| Period | 3 |
| Quotation Mark | 1 |
| Spelling | 2 |

**THURSDAY**　　　　　　　　　　　**WEEK 15**

Name _____

the teachers principles and adults whom allow soda and candy machines point out that the money earned is used to improve the schools. by allowing the machines schools can pay for extra programs? Students will buy junk food anyway" they say. "they should bye it from us because we will use the money on the school" that logic i believe. Sends the wrong message to the students. That message to the students are "Money is the most importnt thing in the world

WATCH FOR
• quotes

**WEDNESDAY**                                    **WEEK 15**

While its true that money is neccesary for a school to run. principles school districts and others cant depend on soda and vending machines. Their presence say to the students "don't pay attention to what we teach you about nutrition give us money! The solution i believe is a compromise Soda and vending machines may be allowed but they should be available only at certain times. other machines however should offer milk fresh fruit and other healthy foods?

WATCH FOR
• quotes

**THURSDAY**                                     **WEEK 15**

Preview the 4 daily lessons to ensure you review or introduce skills that may be unfamiliar to students.

# Kitty's Diary

January 1, 1828

dear diary

It's snowing! The tree's outside our cabin look like they've been dipped in sugar this is our first new years day in Kentucky We lived in virginia before but papa said, Brother it's getting too crowded here!" We will stay close to the warm hearth on this cold winter day. Boy, am i glad we got the roof on!

| Error Summary | |
|---|---|
| Capitalization | 9 |
| Punctuation: | |
| Apostrophe | 3 |
| Comma | 6 |
| Period | 2 |
| Quotation Mark | 1 |
| Spelling | 2 |

**MONDAY**　　　　　　　　**WEEK 16**

march 5, 1828

dear diary

Papa and Jim my Brother are out in the woods cutting trees? papa says we need an other acre cleared so we can plant Corn Mama is roasting delicious fresh bear meat. Jim will say "mama, thank you for cooking! All the work has made me hungry." I wonder what he will say about the johnnycake I made by myself? i hope it isnt as hard as the wood he's been cutting!

| Error Summary | |
|---|---|
| Capitalization | 8 |
| Language Usage | 2 |
| Punctuation: | |
| Apostrophe | 1 |
| Comma | 7 |
| Period | 2 |
| Spelling | 1 |

**TUESDAY**　　　　　　　　**WEEK 16**

Name _____

# Kitty's Diary

January, 1 1828

dear diary

    Its snowing! The tree's outside our cabin look like theyve been dipped in sugar this is our first new years day in Kentucky We lived in virginia before but papa said, Brother it's getting to crowded here!" We will stay close to the warm hearth on this cold winter day. Boy am i glad we got the roof on!

WATCH FOR

- salutations
- names of places
- names of holidays
- quotes

**MONDAY**        **WEEK 16**

march 5 1828

dear diary

    Papa and Jim my Brother are out in the woods cutting trees? papa says we need an other acre cleared so we can plant Corn Mama is roasted delicious fresh bear meat. Jim will say "mama thank you for cooking! All the work has make me hungry." I wonder what he will say about the johnnycake I made by myself? i hope it isnt as hard as the wood he's been cutting!

WATCH FOR

- salutations
- quotes

**TUESDAY**        **WEEK 16**

june 10 1828

dear diary

how do weeds grow so fast? It seems that all

Jim and i do is take our hoes and chop weeds out

of the corn patch? Kitty I'd rather go fishing in the

creek! Jim told me. "If you want me to make more

johnnycake, Jim," I told him, "Then you had better

finish ~~you're~~ your rows!" I know our corn crop is going to

be good, Jim and ~~me~~ I havent allowed the weeds to

~~creap~~ creep up on us.

| Error Summary | |
|---|---|
| Capitalization | 6 |
| Language Usage | 1 |
| **Punctuation:** | |
| Apostrophe | 1 |
| Comma | 5 |
| Period | 3 |
| Quotation Mark | 2 |
| Other | 1 |
| Spelling | 2 |

**WEDNESDAY**　　　　　　　**WEEK 16**

november 29 1828

Dear diary

Mama and ~~me~~ I made ~~candels~~ candles today. We melted

tallow, and then dipped strings, called wicks, into the

hot fat then we ~~sit~~ set the wicks a side to cool and

harden. Again and again we dipped the wicks into

the tallow. mama looked at my candles and said,

"Kitty you have made nice fat candles." Now well have

plenty of light when aunt rachel Mama's sister comes

~~too~~ to visit?

| Error Summary | |
|---|---|
| Capitalization | 6 |
| Language Usage | 2 |
| **Punctuation:** | |
| Apostrophe | 1 |
| Comma | 5 |
| Period | 2 |
| Quotation Mark | 1 |
| Spelling | 3 |

**THURSDAY**　　　　　　　**WEEK 16**

Name _____

june 10 1828.

dear diary

    how do weeds grow so fast. It seems that all Jim and i do is take our hoes and chop weeds out of the corn patch? Kitty I'd rather go fishing in the creek! Jim told me. "If you want me to make more johnnycake Jim," I told him "Then you had better finish you're rows!" I know our corn crop is going to be good, Jim and me havent allowed the weeds to creap up on us.

**WATCH FOR**

• salutations
• question marks
• quotes

**WEDNESDAY**                                    **WEEK 16**

november 29 1828

Dear diary

    Mama and me made candels today. We melted tallow, and then dipped strings, called wicks, into the hot fat then we sit the wicks a side to cool and harden. Again and again we dipped the wicks into the tallow. mama looked at my candles and said, Kitty you have made nice fat candles." Now well have plenty of light when aunt rachel Mama's sister comes too visit?

**WATCH FOR**

• salutations
• quotes

**THURSDAY**                                    **WEEK 16**

Preview the 4 daily lessons to ensure you review or introduce skills that may be unfamiliar to students.

# Safe Surfing

surfing isnt just ~~a~~ an ocean sport anymore Instead of using surfboards kid's are using computers and phone lines. instead of surfing wave's kids are surfing the Internet there are safety rules for ocean surfing and ~~they're~~ there are also safety ~~rule~~ rules for internet surfing. Just as you shouldnt surf in the ocean with out following safety rules; you shouldnt surf on the internet without following safety rules. different types of sharks are everywhere!

| Error Summary | |
|---|---|
| Capitalization | 6 |
| Language Usage | 2 |
| Punctuation: | |
| Apostrophe | 3 |
| Comma | 4 |
| Period | 2 |
| Other | 1 |
| Spelling | 4 |

**MONDAY**                                **WEEK 17**

Whether
~~Wether~~ on the ocean or on the Internet, you should never surf alone Before you go online let your parents know what ~~your~~ you're doing. Its a good idea to have your parents do a little surfing with you they may learn something from you and you may learn something from them. They've been screening telemarketers calls for years! Keeping your ~~personnal~~ personal information private is very ~~importent~~ important. Your password real name address and phone number should never be given out

| Error Summary | |
|---|---|
| Capitalization | 1 |
| Punctuation: | |
| Apostrophe | 3 |
| Comma | 5 |
| Period | 3 |
| Spelling | 4 |

**TUESDAY**                               **WEEK 17**

Name _____

# Safe Surfing

surfing isnt just a ocean sport anymore Instead of using surfboards kid's are using computers and phone lines. instead of surfing wave's kids are surfing the Internet there are safety rules for ocean surfing and they're are also safety rule for internet surfing. Just as you shouldnt surf in the ocean with out following safety rules; you shouldnt surf on the internet without following safety rules. different types of sharks are everywhere

- commas
- exclamation points

**MONDAY**                                        **WEEK 17**

Wether on the ocean or on the Internet, you should never surf alone Before you go online let your parents know what your doing. Its a good idea to have your parents do a little surfing with you they may learn something from you and you may learn something from them. Theyve been screening telemarketers calls for years! Keeping your personnal information private is very importent. Your password real name address and phone number should never be given out

- commas
- apostrophes

**TUESDAY**                                       **WEEK 17**

　　　　chat rooms can be a great way to exchange
ideas
~~idea~~ with people you dont ~~no~~ but its very important
　　　　　　　　　　　　　　　　know
your
to keep ~~you're~~ identity a secret. In any chat room,

its important to be respectful of others views,

but offensive messages, called "flames" should never

be tolerated. If you are "flamed" play it safe and

use the "back" button. Question everything on the

internet? many Web sites are reliable, But others have

false or misleading information. Make sure the facts
　　　　　　　　　　　　　　　　　　　sites
can be matched on other ~~cites~~.

**Error Summary**

| | |
|---|---|
| Capitalization | 4 |
| Language Usage | 1 |
| Punctuation: | |
|   Apostrophe | 4 |
|   Comma | 5 |
|   Period | 1 |
| Spelling | 3 |

**WEDNESDAY**　　　　　　　　　　　　**WEEK 17**

　　　　to keep yourself safe you should never agree to

meet someone you have met online in person without

asking your parents first. if you do want to meet

someone face to face be sure to meet in a public

place. And bring a parent along. if this person is
　　　　your　　friend
truly ~~you're freind~~ he or she will want you to be

safe Its important to be cautious because it is easy

to pretend to be someone else Online. The Internet

can be an important link to the world, but surfing the
　　　　safely
world ~~safe~~ is important, too.

**Error Summary**

| | |
|---|---|
| Capitalization | 5 |
| Language Usage | 1 |
| Punctuation: | |
|   Apostrophe | 1 |
|   Comma | 4 |
|   Period | 3 |
| Spelling | 3 |

**THURSDAY**　　　　　　　　　　　　**WEEK 17**

　　　　EMC 2729 • Daily Paragraph Editing, Grade 6 • ©2004 by Evan-Moor Corp.

Name _____

chat rooms can be a great way to exchange idea with people you dont no but its very important to keep you're identity a secret. In any chat room its' important to be respectful of others views, but offensive messages, called "flames" should never be tolerated. If you are "flamed" play it safe and use the "back" button. Question everything on the internet? many Web sites are reliable. But others have false or misleading information. Make sure the facts can be matched on other cites.

- commas
- apostrophes

**WEDNESDAY**                                        **WEEK 17**

to keep yourself safe you should never agree to meet someone you have met online in person without asking your parent's first. if you do want to meet someone face to face be sure to meet in a public place. And bring a parent along. if this person is truly you're freind he or she will want you to be safe Its important to be cautious because it is easy to pretend to be someone else Online. The Internet can be an important link to the world; but surfing the world safe is important, too

- commas
- apostrophes

**THURSDAY**                                        **WEEK 17**

Preview the 4 daily lessons to ensure you review or introduce skills that may be unfamiliar to students.

# High-Altitude Cooking

A mountain climber hungry and chilled wants to cook pasta potatoes and eggs for dinner. high on the mountain she starts her stove. when the water starts boiling she puts in her food. When she ~~think~~ thinks it has cooked long enough she takes a bite. "this food is raw! she ~~crys~~ cries and she spits it out Why was it raw? She cooked it for the same amount of time She uses back home in her snug cozy house on the beach

| Error Summary | |
|---|---|
| Capitalization | 4 |
| Language Usage | 1 |
| Punctuation: | |
|   Comma | 9 |
|   Period | 3 |
|   Quotation Mark | 1 |
|   Other | 1 |
| Spelling | 2 |

**MONDAY**      **WEEK 18**

the climber didnt think about the difference in atmospheric pressure the atmosphere of air surrounding Earth creates pressure against us. As we go higher air gets thinner and the thinner air exerts less pressure. When the air is thinner it takes less energy to boil water. At sea level the temperature of boiling water is 212°F or 100°C but as we go higher the ~~temperture~~ temperature at which water boils decreases. it ~~take~~ takes longer to cook pasta eggs and other foods

| Error Summary | |
|---|---|
| Capitalization | 3 |
| Language Usage | 1 |
| Punctuation: | |
|   Apostrophe | 1 |
|   Comma | 8 |
|   Period | 2 |
| Spelling | 1 |

**TUESDAY**      **WEEK 18**

Name _____

# High-Altitude Cooking

WATCH FOR

A mountain climber hungry and chilled wants to cook pasta potatos and eggs for dinner. high on the mountain she starts her stove. when the water starts boiling she puts in her food. When she think it has cooked long enough she takes a bite. "this food is raw! she crys and she spits it out Why was it raw. She cooked it for the same amount of time. She uses back home in her snug cozy house on the beach

- commas
- quotes

**MONDAY**                                              **WEEK 18**

---

the climber didnt think about the difference in atmospheric pressure the atmosphere of air surrounding Earth creates pressure against us. As we go higher air gets thinner and the thinner air exerts less pressure. When the air is thinner it takes less energy to boil water. At sea level the temperature of boiling water is 212°F or 100°C but as we go higher the temperture at which water boils decreases. it take longer to cook pasta eggs and other foods

WATCH FOR

- commas

**TUESDAY**                                              **WEEK 18**

as a general rule of thumb the temperture
for boiling water decreases by 1°F for every
540 feet of altitude (0.56°C for every 165 meters)
The mountain climber hungry and chilled could not
change the temperature at witch water boiled but
she could change her cooking time. To make up for
the lower boiling temperature she needed to cook her
potatoes pasta and eggs longer Time and temperature
is what matter when it come to cooking, Not weather
water is boiling.

*(margin corrections: temperature; which; are; comes; whether)*

| Error Summary | |
|---|---|
| Capitalization | 2 |
| Language Usage | 2 |
| Punctuation: | |
|    Comma | 7 |
|    Period | 2 |
| Spelling | 3 |

**WEDNESDAY**　　　　　　**WEEK 18**

the mountain climber hungry and tired returned
home She reads a cookbook and learned how
atmospheric pressure affects cooking time. why I
can cook even faster in my bright cheerful kitchen
she said. With a pressure cooker I can make water
boil at a higher temperature" Rather than decrease
pressure Pressure cookers apply pressure. They can
raise the boiling temperature of water to 250°F
(121°C) That way, noodles rice and other foods take
less time to cook

*(margin corrections: read; why)*

| Error Summary | |
|---|---|
| Capitalization | 3 |
| Language Usage | 1 |
| Punctuation: | |
|    Comma | 9 |
|    Period | 4 |
|    Quotation Mark | 3 |

**THURSDAY**　　　　　　**WEEK 18**

Name _____          83

as a general rule of thumb the temperture for boiling water decreases by 1°F for every 540 feet of altitude (0.56°C for every 165 meters) The mountain climber hungry and chilled could not change the temperature at witch water boiled but she could change her cooking time. To make up for the lower boiling temperature she needed to cook her potatoes pasta and eggs longer Time and temperature is what matter when it come to cooking, Not weather water is boiling.

WATCH FOR

• commas

**WEDNESDAY**                                    **WEEK 18**

the mountain climber hungry and tired returned home She reads a cookbook and learned how atmospheric pressure affects cooking time. why I can cook even faster in my bright cheerful kitchen she said. With a pressure cooker I can make water boil at a higher temperature" Rather than decrease pressure. Pressure cookers apply pressure. They can raise the boiling temperature of water to 250°F (121°C) That way, noodles rice and other foods take less time to cook

WATCH FOR

• commas
• quotes

**THURSDAY**                                     **WEEK 18**

Preview the 4 daily lessons to ensure you review or introduce skills that may be unfamiliar to students.

# Marian Anderson's Gift of Song

Marian Anderson a gifted African-American singer was born in 1897 when marian was growing up african americans were discriminated against many public places were segregated. Marian couldn't enroll in music school because of her color but she wouldn't allow her voice to be silenced. Marian went on to become the first african american to sing a major role at the metropolitan opera house in New York city.

### Error Summary

| | |
|---|---|
| Capitalization | 11 |
| Punctuation: | |
| Apostrophe | 2 |
| Comma | 4 |
| Period | 2 |

**MONDAY**                                    **WEEK 19**

When she was only six years old marian joined her church's junior choir. After a few years she was singing in both the junior and the senior choirs she sang for other ~~churchs~~ churches on special ~~ocasions~~ occasions, too. Marians parents wanted to give marian music lessons, but they couldn't afford them. Marian's Father died when she was young? Marian her sister and her mother moved to her Grandparents house marian's mother ~~clean~~ cleaned houses and washed clothes to support the family

### Error Summary

| | |
|---|---|
| Capitalization | 6 |
| Language Usage | 1 |
| Punctuation: | |
| Apostrophe | 3 |
| Comma | 5 |
| Period | 4 |
| Spelling | 2 |

**TUESDAY**                                    **WEEK 19**

Name _____

# Marian Anderson's Gift of Song

Marian Anderson a gifted African-American singer was born in 1897 when marian was growing up african americans were discriminated against many public places were segregated. Marian couldnt enroll in music school because of her color but she wouldnt allow her voice to be silenced. Marian went on to become the first african american to sing a major role at the metropolitan opera house in New York city.

WATCH FOR

- names of people
- names of ethnic groups
- names of places

**MONDAY**　　　　　　　　　　　　**WEEK 19**

When she was only six years old marian joined her church's junior choir. After a few years she was singing in both the junior and the senior choirs she sang for other churchs on special ocasions, too. Marians parents wanted to give marian music lessons. but they couldnt afford them. Marian's Father died when she was young? Marian her sister and her mother moved to her Grandparents house marian's mother clean houses and washed clothes to support the family

WATCH FOR

- names of people
- commas

**TUESDAY**　　　　　　　　　　　　**WEEK 19**

marian was not allowed into music school because of her color, but she was determined to take lessons. With money she earned singing, she helped pay for her own lessons. Marians church helped pay for lessons, too, to one teacher even gave Marian free lessons. When Marian traveled by train to sing in georgia she had to sit in a car for african americans. She couldnt eat in the dining car. In new york city, Marian had to stay in hotel's for African Americans.

**Error Summary**

| | |
|---|---|
| Capitalization | 8 |
| Punctuation: | |
| Apostrophe | 2 |
| Comma | 3 |
| Period | 3 |
| Spelling | 2 |

**WEDNESDAY**                                                           **WEEK 19**

---

Marian went to europe where she became very famous marian could sing in europe, but she couldnt sing in public halls in Washington DC, her nations capital. This made people angry, then the government of the united states invited Marian to sing on the steps of the lincoln memorial. more than 75,000 people, Black and White, sat together. they listened to Marian sing. Later, Marian sang at the white house. She died in 1993. She is still remembered for her determination, courage, and amazing voice.

**Error Summary**

| | |
|---|---|
| Capitalization | 14 |
| Punctuation: | |
| Apostrophe | 2 |
| Comma | 6 |
| Period | 7 |
| Spelling | 2 |

**THURSDAY**                                                           **WEEK 19**

Name _____

marian was not allowed into music school because of her color but she was determined to take lessons. With money she earned singing she helped pay for her own lessons. Marians church helped pay for lessons, to? one teacher even gave Marian free lessons When Marian traveled by train to sing in georgia she had to sit in a car for african americans. She couldnt eat in the dining car. In new york city, Marian had to stay in hotel's for African Americans

- names of people
- names of ethnic groups
- names of places

**WEDNESDAY**                    **WEEK 19**

Marian went to europe where she became very famoes marian could sing in europe but she couldnt sing in public halls in Washington DC, her nations capital. This made people angry then the goverment of the united states invited Marian to sing on the steps of the lincoln memorial. more than 75,000 people Black and White sat together. they listened to Marian sing? Later, Marian sang at the white house. She died in 1993, She is still remembered for her determination courage and amazing voice

- names of people
- names of places
- abbreviations

**THURSDAY**                    **WEEK 19**

Preview the 4 daily lessons to ensure you review or introduce skills that may be unfamiliar to students.

# Manatees

the Manatee often known as the "sea cow" is a gentle, giant sea creature that has been floating around for 60 Million years. A warmblooded mammal, the Manatee must travel to survive. many manatees live near Kings bay Florida. In the summer, they leave florida and head to the gulf of Mexico. for millions of years, the manatees' survival depended only on finding warm waters. Unfortunately, humans are now their greatest threat.

| Error Summary | |
|---|---|
| Capitalization | 9 |
| Punctuation: | |
| Apostrophe | 1 |
| Comma | 5 |
| Period | 4 |
| Spelling | 3 |

**MONDAY**                                **WEEK 20**

Boating accidents are the greatest cause of death for manatees. Today. a manatee is a mammal, so it must come to the surface to breathe air. This means that every five to six minutes the manatee is in danger of being caught in speedboats' propellers. Most adult manatees have scars from propellers. human pollution is a threat to manatees, too. Due to this pollution, a deadly plant, Red Tide, has flourished in the gulf of mexico. many manatees have died because of this plant.

| Error Summary | |
|---|---|
| Capitalization | 8 |
| Punctuation: | |
| Apostrophe | 1 |
| Comma | 3 |
| Period | 4 |
| Spelling | 1 |

**TUESDAY**                                **WEEK 20**

Name _____

# Manatees

the Manatee often known as the "sea cow" is a gentle giant sea creature that has been floating around for 60 Million years A warmblooded mammal, the Manatee must travel to survive many manatees live near Kings bay Florida. In the summer, they leave florida and head to the gulf of Mexico for millions of years the manatees survival depended only on finding warm waters Unfortuneately, humans are now there greatest thret.

**MONDAY**                                              **WEEK 20**

Boating accidents are the greatest cause of death for manatees. Today. a manatee is a mammal so it must come to the surface to breath air. This means that every five to six minutes the manatee is in danger of being caught in speedboats propellers. Most adult manatees have scars from propellers? human pollution is a threat to manatees, too. Due to this pollution, a deadly plant Red Tide has flourished in the gulf of mexico many manatees have died because of this plant

**TUESDAY**                                             **WEEK 20**

Manatee mothers give birth to one baby every two to five years, but sometimes, like humans, a manatee can have twins. A mother manatee must help her calf learn how to ~~breath~~ breathe, so at first she may keep her calf near the surface of the water. Calves stay with their mother's for one to two years. during this time, they learn where to find food and where to migrate. when a baby manatee is born, it weighs 34 to 43 kilos (75 to 95 lbs). It reaches 453 to 544 kilos (1,000 to 1,200 lbs). in just ~~for~~ four to five years.

### Error Summary

| Capitalization | 2 |
|---|---|
| Punctuation: | |
| Comma | 5 |
| Period | 5 |
| Spelling | 3 |

**WEDNESDAY**                    **WEEK 20**

manatees need about 150 pounds of food each day. their diet consists of water plants. Genuine gentle giants, manatees do not have the same advantages as many other creatures of the sea. They aren't fast, and they don't have sharp teeth. some people are working hard to help the manatees. speed limits have been set so manatees can get away from speedboats. In some waterways, speedboat's have only limited access. with help from humans, the manatee ~~mite~~ might live another 60 million years.

### Error Summary

| Capitalization | 5 |
|---|---|
| Punctuation: | |
| Apostrophe | 2 |
| Comma | 2 |
| Period | 6 |
| Spelling | 2 |

**THURSDAY**                    **WEEK 20**

Name _____

Manatee mothers give birth to one baby every two to five years but sometimes like humans a manatee can have twins. A mother manatee must help her calf learn how to breath so at first she may keep her calf near the surface of the water. Calves stay with their mother's for one to two years during this time, they learn where to find food and where to migrate when a baby manatee is born it weighs 34 to 43 kilos (75 to 95 lbs) It reaches 453 to 544 kilos (1,000 to 1,200 lbs). in just for to five years.

WATCH FOR

- commas
- abbreviations

**WEDNESDAY**                                    **WEEK 20**

manatees need about 150 pounds of food each day their diet consists of water plants? Genuine gentle giants, manatees do not have the same advantages as many other creatures of the sea. They arent fast and they dont have sharp teeth some people are working hard to help the manatees speed limits have been set so manatees can get away from speedboats. In some waterways, speedboat's have only limited access with help from humans the manatee mite live another 60 million years

WATCH FOR

- commas

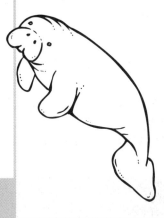

**THURSDAY**                                    **WEEK 20**

Preview the 4 daily lessons to ensure you review or introduce skills that may be unfamiliar to students.

# An Exciting Adventure

When i joined the peace corps, I was sent to belize a small country in central america. I was going to teach at a boys' school. The school was far down a dirt road, and the wooden buildings were built on stilts because it rained so much. The boys lived at the school, and they ~~raise~~ raised rabbits, grew ~~vegetables~~ vegetables and ~~studyed~~ studied hard. we ate lots of rice and beans, and sometimes the boys would catch ~~a~~ an iguana, or "bamboo chicken," to eat.

### Error Summary

| | |
|---|---|
| Capitalization | 7 |
| Language Usage | 2 |
| Punctuation: | |
| Apostrophe | 1 |
| Comma | 7 |
| Period | 2 |
| Quotation Mark | 1 |
| Spelling | 2 |

**MONDAY**                                **WEEK 21**

---

the peace corps was established on march 1, 1961. Volunteers from the Education, Health, Environment, Business, and agriculture fields have served in over 136 ~~countrys~~ countries. when I was a volunteer, I ~~drinked~~ drank rainwater collected in a cistern. My tiny, simple house didnt have hot water, but i was lucky to have cold water. Long trails of ants would come into my house, but I liked them because they carried away the dead cockroaches. I wasnt as pleased about the scorpion or the snake I found!

### Error Summary

| | |
|---|---|
| Capitalization | 10 |
| Language Usage | 1 |
| Punctuation: | |
| Apostrophe | 2 |
| Comma | 9 |
| Period | 2 |
| Spelling | 1 |

**TUESDAY**                                **WEEK 21**

Name _____

# An Exciting Adventure

When i joined the peace corps. I was sent to belize a small country in central america. I was going to teach at a boys school The school was far down a dirt road and the wooden buildings were built on stilts because it rained so much. The boys lived at the school and they raise rabbits grew vegtables and studied hard. we ate lots of rice and beans and sometimes the boys would catch a iguana, or "bamboo chicken, to eat

WATCH FOR

• names of organizations
• names of countries
• names of regions
• special words in quotes

**MONDAY**                                    **WEEK 21**

the peace corps was established on march 1 1961. Volunteers from the Education Health Environment Business and agriculture fields have served in over 136 countrys. when I was a volunteer I drinked rainwater collected in a cistern My tiny simple house didnt have hot water but i was lucky to have cold water Long trails of ants would come into my house but I liked them because they carried away the dead cockroaches. I wasnt as pleased about the scorpion or the snake I found!

WATCH FOR

• names of organizations
• commas

**TUESDAY**                                    **WEEK 21**

On really hot days i would take the boys down to the big river that bordered the school. One of the boys was a good fast swimmer I asked him how he had become such a good swimmer? This boy had grown ~~grew~~ up on a cay a low island or reef of sand or coral, along Belizes Barrier reef. "miss" he said "my father would take me out on his boat and I would help him with his traps. I learned how to ~~too~~ swim fast because there are sharks in the water!

**Error Summary**

| | |
|---|---|
| Capitalization | 5 |
| Language Usage | 1 |
| Punctuation: | |
| Apostrophe | 1 |
| Comma | 6 |
| Period | 2 |
| Quotation Mark | 1 |
| Spelling | 1 |

**WEDNESDAY**                                    **WEEK 21**

a tropical country belize is hot and humid. At first, it was hard to get used to the heat but soon it seemed normal one day, it dropped down to a chilly 70°F and i saw a dog shivering uncontrollably. I couldnt laugh at it because I was wearing a sweater! The Peace Corps was a wonderful exciting adventure and before I knew it my two ~~too~~ years of service were ~~was~~ over. "Yes I tell everyone who asks "you should join the peace corps. It will be ~~was~~ the toughest job youll ever love.

**Error Summary**

| | |
|---|---|
| Capitalization | 6 |
| Language Usage | 2 |
| Punctuation: | |
| Apostrophe | 2 |
| Comma | 8 |
| Period | 2 |
| Quotation Mark | 2 |
| Spelling | 1 |

**THURSDAY**                                    **WEEK 21**

Name _____

On really hot days i would take the boys down to the big river that bordered the school. One of the boys was a good fast swimmer I asked him how he had become such a good swimmer? This boy had grew up on a cay a low island or reef of sand or coral, along Belizes Barrier reef. "miss" he said "my Father would take me out on his boat and I would help him with his traps. I learned how too swim fast because there are Sharks in the water!

**WEDNESDAY**                                    **WEEK 21**

a tropical country belize is hot and humid. At first, it was hard to get used to the heat but soon it seemed normal one day, it dropped down to a chilly 70°F and i saw a dog shivering uncontrollably. I couldnt laugh at it because I was wearing a sweater! The Peace Corps was a wonderful exciting adventure and before I knew it my too years of service was over. "Yes I tell everyone who asks "you should join the peace corps. It was the toughest job youll ever love

**THURSDAY**                                    **WEEK 21**

Preview the 4 daily lessons to ensure you review or introduce skills that may be unfamiliar to students.

# Hull House Diary

july 7 1897

dear diary,

we took the train to chicago illinois, today. Carrying every thing we owned we walks to hull house. Mama said do you think shell help? i dont want no more dissappointments." we heard that jane addams, the lady who started Hull House helps immigrants Oh I do hope she can help papa find a job

**Error Summary**

| Capitalization | 14 |
|---|---|
| Language Usage | 2 |
| Punctuation: | |
| Apostrophe | 2 |
| Comma | 7 |
| Period | 3 |
| Quotation Mark | 1 |
| Other | 1 |
| Spelling | 2 |

**MONDAY**　　　　**WEEK 22**

july 14 1897

Dear diary,

My Ive never seen a place like this hull house before. Miss Addams a social reformer starts this settlement house in 1889. we didnt expect no help but Miss Addams helps everyone. Mama asked, "did you know she started the first public baths in chicago? while helping in hull Houses kitchen i heard that miss addams is even investigating why the garbage is never picked up

**Error Summary**

| Capitalization | 13 |
|---|---|
| Language Usage | 2 |
| Punctuation: | |
| Apostrophe | 3 |
| Comma | 8 |
| Period | 3 |
| Quotation Mark | 1 |

**TUESDAY**　　　　**WEEK 22**

Name _____

# Hull House Diary

july 7 1897.

dear diary;

we took the train to chicago illinois, today. Carrying every thing we owned we walks to hull house. Mama said do you think shell help i dont want no more dissappointments." we heard that jane addams, the lady who started Hull House helps immigrants Oh I do hope she can help papa find a job

**WATCH FOR**
- salutations
- names of people
- names of places
- quotes

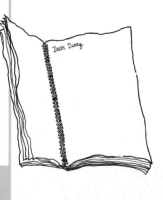

| MONDAY | WEEK 22 |
| --- | --- |

---

july 14. 1897

Dear diary

My Ive never seen a place like this hull house before. Miss. Addams a social reformer starts this settlement house in 1889. we didnt expect no help but Miss. Addams helps everyone. Mama asked "did you know she started the first public baths in chicago? while helping in hull Houses Kitchen i heard that miss addams is even investigating why the garbage is never picked up

**WATCH FOR**
- salutations
- names of people
- names of places
- quotes

| TUESDAY | WEEK 22 |
| --- | --- |

july 21, 1897

dear Diary,

Hooray! papa starts painting in the factory today, and mama has clothes to sew at home. my oldest brother Frank is selling newspapers. after miss addams helped both my Mama and Papa find work, papa said, wow! Ive never met no lady like this before." Miss Addams started chicagos first public kitchen, playground, and swimming pool, and she is truly An amazing lady.

**Error Summary**

| | |
|---|---|
| Capitalization | 14 |
| Language Usage | 1 |
| Punctuation: | |
| Apostrophe | 2 |
| Comma | 9 |
| Period | 2 |
| Quotation Mark | 1 |
| Other | 2 |

**WEDNESDAY**                    **WEEK 22**

july 28, 1897

dear diary,

I didnt want no Doctor to look at me, but Miss Addams says everyone should be checked for Tuberculosis. The doctor also a immigrant, said, dont you want to be healthy in your new country?" My Im glad that I dont have tuberculosis. After watching the doctor work, I decides that one day I would like to be a Doctor. Just like miss Addams, i could help people.

**Error Summary**

| | |
|---|---|
| Capitalization | 9 |
| Language Usage | 3 |
| Punctuation: | |
| Apostrophe | 4 |
| Comma | 9 |
| Period | 2 |
| Quotation Mark | 1 |
| Other | 1 |
| Spelling | 2 |

**THURSDAY**                    **WEEK 22**

Name _____

july 21 1897

dear Diary

    Hooray papa starts painting in the factory today and mama has clothes to sew at home. my oldest brother Frank is selling newspapers. after miss addams helped both my Mama and Papa find work, papa said wow Ive never met no lady like this before." Miss. Addams started chicagos first public kitchen playground and swimming pool and she is truly. An amazing lady.

**WATCH FOR**

- salutations
- names of people
- names of places
- exclamation points

---

**WEDNESDAY**                                         **WEEK 22**

july, 28, 1897

dear diary

    I didnt want no Doctor to look at me but Miss. Addams says everyone should be checked for Tuberculosis. The doctor also a immigrant said dont you want to be healthy in your new country" My Im glad that I dont have tuberculosis. After watching the doctor work. I decides that one day I would like to be a Doctor. Just like miss Addams' i could help peopel

**WATCH FOR**

- salutations
- names of people
- quotes

---

**THURSDAY**                                           **WEEK 22**

Preview the 4 daily lessons to ensure you review or introduce skills that may be unfamiliar to students.

# Pecos Bill

youve heard about pecos bill the texas wrangler. as tall as a house and as ~~stronger~~ strong as an ox Bill was raised by coyotes. When it ~~is~~ time to round up his cattle bill would point his nose toward the bright open sky and he would let out a coyote howl. the howl would scare the cattle and ~~he~~ they would stampede all the way to abilene If the cattle ever slowed down Bill would just let out another loud wild yell

**Error Summary**

| | |
|---|---|
| Capitalization | 8 |
| Language Usage | 3 |
| Punctuation: | |
|    Apostrophe | 1 |
|    Comma | 8 |
|    Period | 2 |

**MONDAY**             **WEEK 23**

bill could smell almost anything in the air a hundred miles away better head for the cellars" he said one day. Theres a twister coming! Bills men herded the cattle into a tunnel bill had dug out, using Rattler his pet snake as a drill. Bills men then went into the cellar but Bill wouldnt go "Im going to ride this one out he said. Bill and Bulldozer, Bills horse waited for the twister. ugly wild and angry the twister took off after bill. Bulldozer stepped away like a spinning dancing ballerina

**Error Summary**

| | |
|---|---|
| Capitalization | 7 |
| Punctuation: | |
|    Apostrophe | 6 |
|    Comma | 10 |
|    Period | 4 |
|    Quotation Mark | 4 |

**TUESDAY**             **WEEK 23**

Name _____

# Pecos Bill

youve heard about pecos bill the texas wrangler. as tall as a house and as stronger as an ox Bill was raised by coyotes. When it is time to round up his cattle bill would point his nose toward the bright open sky and he would let out a coyote howl. the howl would scare the cattle and he would stampede all the way to abilene If the cattle ever slowed down. Bill would just let out another loud wild yell

- names of people
- names of places
- commas

| MONDAY | WEEK 23 |
|---|---|

bill could smell almost anything in the air a hundred miles away better head for the cellars" he said one day. Theres a twister coming! Bills men herded the cattle into a tunnel bill had dug out, using Rattler his pet Snake as a drill. Bills men then went into the cellar but Bill wouldnt go "Im going to ride this one out he said. Bill and Bulldozer, Bills horse waited for the twister. ugly wild and angry the twister took off after bill. Bulldozer stepped away. Like a spinning dancing ballerina

- names of people
- names of pets
- quotes

| TUESDAY | WEEK 23 |
|---|---|

"I've tamed bears, snakes, and wolves," Bill said to bulldozer his horse. "Wait for me over yonder and I'll take care of this bag-of-wind. Taking out his rope, bill dropped it over the top of the twister. Faster than a bolt of lightning and hanging on like a flea to a dog, Bill climbed to the top of the whirling, spinning twister, the Twister bucked, kicked, and roared but Bill rode it as if he were a kid riding a rocking horse. bill was as calm as a hibernating bear.

**Error Summary**

| | |
|---|---|
| Capitalization | 5 |
| Language Usage | 2 |
| Punctuation: | |
|    Apostrophe | 2 |
|    Comma | 10 |
|    Period | 3 |
|    Quotation Mark | 1 |
| Spelling | 1 |

**WEDNESDAY**                    **WEEK 23**

---

Bill could see houses, cattle, and tools swirling inside the twister. why let this bag-of-wind smash up everything? Bill said. reaching down inside, bill pulled out the houses, cattle, and tools. He tossed them out behind the twister, and the houses landed in a straight row. The cattle landed right on the grass, and the tools landed in the fields. Thanks to Bill, the open, dry stretch of prairie now had a pretty town. the Twister empty and tired, became a little breeze. Bill, as wild as ever, howled like a coyote.

**Error Summary**

| | |
|---|---|
| Capitalization | 5 |
| Language Usage | 1 |
| Punctuation: | |
|    Comma | 13 |
|    Period | 3 |
|    Quotation Mark | 2 |
|    Other | 1 |
| Spelling | 2 |

**THURSDAY**                    **WEEK 23**

EMC 2729 • Daily Paragraph Editing, Grade 6 • ©2004 by Evan-Moor Corp.

Name _____

"Ive tamed bears snakes and wolfes" Bill said to bulldozer his horse. "Wait for me over yonder and Ill take care of this bag-of-wind Taking out his rope bill dropped it over the top of the twister. Faster than a bolt of lightning and hanging on like a flea to a dog Bill climbed to the top of the whirling spinning twister the Twister bucked kicked, and roared but Bill ride it as if he were a kid riding a rocking horse. bill is as calm as a hibernating bear

WATCH FOR

• names of people
• names of pets
• quotes

**WEDNESDAY**          **WEEK 23**

Bill could see houses cattle and tools swirling inside the twister. why let this bag-of-wind smash up everything Bill said. reaching down inside bill pulled out the houses catle and tools He tosses them out behind the twister and the houses landed in a strait row. The cattle landed right on the grass and the tools landed in the fields. Thanks to Bill the open dry stretch of prairie now had a pretty town the Twister empty and tired became a little breeze. Bill as wild as ever howled like a coyote

WATCH FOR

• quotes
• question marks

**THURSDAY**          **WEEK 23**

Preview the 4 daily lessons to ensure you review or introduce skills that may be unfamiliar to students.

# Duct Tape and Warts

Duct Tape has long been known as a solution to almost anything it can fasten NASA equipment together, seal air ducts, cover ripped seats, and stop leaky pipes. recently, Doctors have found a new use for duct tape? In her article Handyman's Hero Hailed as a Healer marian uhlman inquirer staff writer reports on a medical study involving duct tape and warts. She interviewed Dr. Focht, the doctor who performed the study.

| Error Summary | |
|---|---|
| Capitalization | 7 |
| Punctuation: | |
| Comma | 7 |
| Period | 4 |
| Quotation Mark | 2 |
| Other | 1 |
| Spelling | 2 |

**MONDAY**                          **WEEK 24**

Duct tape is more practical for parents and patients to use" says dr focht in the article Handyman's Hero Hailed as a Healer Dr. Focht, the investigator placed a small piece of duct tape on his patients' warts. after wearing the tape for six days, his patients took off the tape then the wart was soaked, scraped, and left to air overnight. The tape was reapplied the next morning, and the treatment continued for up to two months. In 22 of dr Focht's 26 patients, the wart disappeared.

| Error Summary | |
|---|---|
| Capitalization | 5 |
| Language Usage | 1 |
| Punctuation: | |
| Apostrophe | 2 |
| Comma | 8 |
| Period | 5 |
| Quotation Mark | 3 |
| Spelling | 2 |

**TUESDAY**                          **WEEK 24**

Name _____

# Duct Tape and Warts

Duct Tape has long been known as a solution to almost anything it can fasten NASA equipment togeather seal air ducts cover ripped seats and stop leaky pipes. recently, Doctors have found a new use for duct tape? In her article Handyman's Hero Hailed as a Healer marian uhlman inquirer staff writer reports on a medical study involving duct tape and warts. She interviewed Dr Focht the doctor who preformed the study

**WATCH FOR**

- names of people
- names of newspapers
- titles of people
- titles of articles

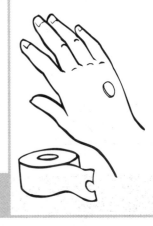

**MONDAY**                                          **WEEK 24**

Duct tape is more practical for parents and patients to use" says dr focht in the article Handyman's Hero Hailed as a Healer Dr Focht the investigater placed a small peace of duct tape on his patients warts. after wearing the tape for six days his patients took off the tape then the wart was soaked scraped and left to air overnight. The tape is reapplied the next morning and the treatment continued for up to two months. In 22 of dr Fochts 26 patients the wart disappeared.

**WATCH FOR**

- titles of people
- titles of articles
- quotes

**TUESDAY**                                          **WEEK 24**

in her article "Handyman's Hero Hailed as a Healer" Uhlman compares Dr. Focht's duct tape patients with those who froze ~~there~~ their warts. "By comparison, just 15 of 25 patients had their warts disappear," Uhlman writes. exactly how duct tape works ~~are~~ is still uncertain but dr. focht feels that it may "involve stimulation of the patient's immune system through ~~threw~~ local irritation" regardless of how it works duct tape is easy cheap and less painful than other wart-removal methods.

### Error Summary

| | |
|---|---|
| Capitalization | 5 |
| Language Usage | 1 |
| **Punctuation:** | |
| Apostrophe | 2 |
| Comma | 6 |
| Period | 4 |
| Quotation Mark | 3 |
| Spelling | 2 |

**WEDNESDAY**  **WEEK 24**

Uhlman interviewed several Doctors for her article "Handyman's Hero Hailed as a Healer." The doctors ~~agread~~ agreed that using duct tape to remove warts was a great idea. Dr. hyde, one of the doctors interviewed, said that the study should be done again. she notes that the patients ranged in age from 3 to 22, and that ~~there~~ their warts were mainly on ~~they're~~ their hands and feet. people have found uses for duct tape while repairing, making, or binding things. Is it any surprise that it's useful in doctors' offices, too?

### Error Summary

| | |
|---|---|
| Capitalization | 5 |
| **Punctuation:** | |
| Apostrophe | 2 |
| Comma | 5 |
| Period | 3 |
| Quotation Mark | 2 |
| Other | 1 |
| Spelling | 3 |

**THURSDAY**  **WEEK 24**

Name _____

in her article Handyman's Hero Hailed as a Healer Uhlman compares Dr Fochts duct tape patients with those who froze there warts. "By comparison, just 15 of 25 patients had their warts disappear Uhlman writes. exactly how duct tape works are still uncertain but dr focht feels that it may "involve stimulation of the patients immune system threw local irritation" regardless of how it works duct tape is easy cheap and less painful than other wart-removal methods

WATCH FOR

- titles of people
- titles of articles
- quotes

**WEDNESDAY**                                    **WEEK 24**

Uhlman interviewed several Doctors for her article Handyman's Hero Hailed as a Healer. The doctors agread that using duct tape to remove warts was a great idea Dr hyde one of the doctors interviewed said that the study should be done again. she notes that the patients ranged in age from 3 to 22. And that there warts were mainly on they're hands and feet. people have found uses for duct tape while repairing making or binding things Is it any surprise that its useful in doctors offices, too

WATCH FOR

- titles of people
- titles of articles
- question marks

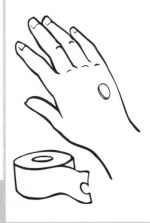

**THURSDAY**                                      **WEEK 24**

Preview the 4 daily lessons to ensure you review or introduce skills that may be unfamiliar to students.

# The Parthenon

The parthenon in athens greece is a~an~ amazing structure. Over 2,400 years old, it has withstood whether~weather~ wars, and public use. The parthenon was original~originally~ built as a temple of worship to the goddess athena. construction began in 480 BC. In the sixth century, christians used the Parthenon as a church, and muslims used it as a mosque in the 1400s. Today, however, the parthenon is a symbol of greek society and vision.

**Error Summary**

| | |
|---|---|
| Capitalization | 10 |
| Language Usage | 2 |
| Punctuation: | |
| Comma | 8 |
| Period | 4 |
| Spelling | 1 |

**MONDAY**                          **WEEK 25**

---

greek architects use~used~ superior building and design skills when they builded~built~ the parthenon. Most buildings at that time were built of wood, but the Parthenon was built with marble. Using a new technique, stones were held together without using mortar. Instead, clamps were embedded in the stones with molten lead to hold the stones together. clay tiles were used for the roof. these tile~tiles~ made the parthenon decorative and rainproof.

**Error Summary**

| | |
|---|---|
| Capitalization | 5 |
| Language Usage | 3 |
| Punctuation: | |
| Comma | 2 |
| Period | 3 |

**TUESDAY**                          **WEEK 25**

Name _____

# The Parthenon

The parthenon in athens greece is a amazing structure. Over 2,400 years old. it has withstood whether wars and public use. The parthenon was original built as a temple of worship to the goddess athena construction began in 480 BC In the sixth century christians used the Parthenon as a church, and muslims used it as a mosque in the 1400s. Today however the parthenon is a symbol of greek society and vision

- names of people
- names of religions
- abbreviations

**MONDAY**                                        **WEEK 25**

---

greek architects use superior building and design skills when they builded the parthenon. Most buildings at that time were built of wood but the Parthenon was built with marble. Using a new technique stones were held together without using mortar. Instead, clamps were embedded in the stones with molten lead to hold the stones together clay tiles were used for the roof these tile made the parthenon decorative and rainproof

- names of places
- names of nationalities

**TUESDAY**                                        **WEEK 25**

The parthenon was ~~solid~~ solidly built but it was also an artistic marvel not one "straight" line on the Parthenon for example is actually straight. Vertical columns in fact appear to be narrower in the middle when they actually are not. the architects of the parthenon adjusted for this by building ~~there~~ their columns with a bulge in the middle. this type of adjustment is called ~~a~~ an optical refinement. The ~~column~~ columns are not ~~strait~~ straight to be sure but they look straight

**Error Summary**

| | |
|---|---|
| Capitalization | 5 |
| Language Usage | 3 |
| Punctuation: | |
| Comma | 7 |
| Period | 2 |
| Spelling | 2 |

**WEDNESDAY**                                    **WEEK 25**

The Architects also made other optical refinements The columns for example ~~we're~~ were built to lean toward the center. When they are built ~~perfect~~ perfectly straight, tall columns appear in fact to lean forward If the parthenons ~~column~~ columns were ~~too~~ to extend up into the sky for one mile they would actually touch each other! The seemingly straight columns are not very ~~strait~~ straight at all Despite it's age most of the parthenon still stands today its "straight" lines continue to pass the test of time

**Error Summary**

| | |
|---|---|
| Capitalization | 4 |
| Language Usage | 2 |
| Punctuation: | |
| Apostrophe | 2 |
| Comma | 6 |
| Period | 5 |
| Quotation Mark | 1 |
| Spelling | 3 |

**THURSDAY**                                    **WEEK 25**

Name _____

The parthenon was solid built but it was also an artistic marvel not one "straight" line on the Parthenon for example is actually straight. Vertical columns in fact appear to be narrower in the middle when they actually are not. the architects of the parthenon adjusted for this by building there columns with a bulge in the middle. this type of adjustment is called a optical refinement. The column are not strait to be sure but they look straight

WATCH FOR
- names of places
- special words in quotes

**WEDNESDAY**                          **WEEK 25**

The Architects also made other optical refinements The columns for example we're built to lean toward the center. When they are built perfect straight, tall columns appear in fact to lean forward If the parthenons column were too extend up into the sky for one mile they would actually touch each other! The seemingly straight columns are not very strait at all? Despite it's age most of the parthenon still stands today its straight" lines continue to pass the test of time

WATCH FOR
- names of places
- special words in quotes

**THURSDAY**                          **WEEK 25**

Preview the 4 daily lessons to ensure you review or introduce skills that may be unfamiliar to students.

# Crossing the Desert

my name is bilal and i was born in 1456 I am
ten years old and I have been a slave for as long
as i can remember. My job ~~are~~ is to help care for the
camels who carry trade goods across the dry blazing
sahara Desert. We travel from the salt mines to
Tombouctu the city where we trade our salt for gold
cloth spices and slaves. the west african empire of
mali is very big and powerful and tombouctu is one of
its most famous ~~citys~~ cities

**Error Summary**

| | |
|---|---|
| Capitalization | 11 |
| Language Usage | 1 |
| Punctuation: | |
| Comma | 8 |
| Period | 2 |
| Spelling | 1 |

**MONDAY**　　　　　**WEEK 26**

---

wearing loose cotton robes ~~who~~ that help me keep cool
i walk on foot across the arid hot desert. I know ~~me~~ my
camels so well that i can pick them out of a large
herd. if ~~it~~ they wander off I can follow their tracks. I
like camels Because they can survive in the ~~dessert~~ desert.
When the wind blows camels can close ~~they're~~ their nostrils
to stop the sand from getting in Their feet ~~is~~ are flat
big and round like a plate so they don't sink into the
sand. A camels body ~~temperture~~ temperature can rise 6 degrees
Fahrenheit without doing any harm

**Error Summary**

| | |
|---|---|
| Capitalization | 5 |
| Language Usage | 4 |
| Punctuation: | |
| Apostrophe | 1 |
| Comma | 7 |
| Period | 3 |
| Spelling | 3 |

**TUESDAY**　　　　　**WEEK 26**

Name —————————————————

# Crossing the Desert

my name is bilal and i was born in 1456 I am ten years old and I have been a slave for as long as i can remember. My job are to help care for the camels who carry trade goods across the dry blazing sahara Desert. We travel from the salt mines to Tombouctu. The city where we trade our salt for gold cloth spices and slaves. the west african empire of mali is very big and powerful and tombouctu is one of its most famous citys

- names of people
- names of places
- commas

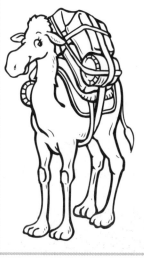

**MONDAY**                                    **WEEK 26**

wearing loose cotton robes who help me keep cool i walk on foot across the arid hot desert. I know me camels so well that i can pick them out of a large herd. if it wander off I can follow their tracks. I like camels. Because they can survive in the dessert. When the wind blows camels can close they're nostrils to stop the sand from getting in Their feet is flat big and round like a plate so they don't sink into the sand. A camels body temperture can rise 6 degrees Fahrenheit without doing any harm

- commas

**TUESDAY**                                    **WEEK 26**

many people think that a camels hump is filled
with water but i know this isnt true A camel stores
fat in its hump and it uses this fat as a ~~sorce~~ source of
energy. tombouctu ~~lays~~ lies just north of the great bend
of the niger river. There is a ~~famos~~ famous university, a
library and a mosque in the city Only the leading
islamic scholars teach at the university and they have
come from all over the world. Started by Tuareg
Nomads in the late eleventh century tombouctu has
~~groan~~ grown to be a busy noisy market.

| Error Summary | |
|---|---|
| Capitalization | 8 |
| Language Usage | 1 |
| Punctuation: | |
|   Apostrophe | 2 |
|   Comma | 7 |
|   Period | 3 |
| Spelling | 3 |

**WEDNESDAY**      **WEEK 26**

When we ~~finaly~~ finally reach tombouctu my camels ~~is~~ are
very thirsty They can drink as much as 35 ~~gallon~~ gallons
of water in less ~~then~~ than six minutes. sometimes, after
i have fed, watered, and cared for my camels, I can
wander ~~threw~~ through the streets of this thriving, bustling city
most of the ~~woman~~ women have their faces covered, but its
different with the tuareg nomads. While Tuareg women
walk around with uncovered faces, Tuareg men carefully
keep their faces covered.

| Error Summary | |
|---|---|
| Capitalization | 5 |
| Language Usage | 3 |
| Punctuation: | |
|   Apostrophe | 1 |
|   Comma | 7 |
|   Period | 3 |
| Spelling | 3 |

**THURSDAY**      **WEEK 26**

EMC 2729 • Daily Paragraph Editing, Grade 6 • ©2004 by Evan-Moor Corp.

Name _____

many people think that a camels hump is filled with water but i know this isnt true A camel stores fat in its hump and it uses this fat as a sorce of energy. tombouctu lays just north of the great bend of the niger river. There is a famos university a library and a mosque in the city Only the leading islamic scholars teach at the university and they have come from all over the world. Started by Tuareg Nomads in the late eleventh century tombouctu has groan to be a busy noisy market

- names of places
- names of religions
- commas

**WEDNESDAY**                                         **WEEK 26**

When we finaly reach tombouctu my camels is very thirsty They can drink as much as 35 gallon of water in less then six minutes. sometimes, after i have fed watered and cared for my camels I can wander threw the streets of this thriving bustling city most of the woman have their faces covered but its different with the tuareg nomads. While Tuareg women walk around with uncovered faces Tuareg men carefully keep their faces covered

- names of ethnic groups
- commas

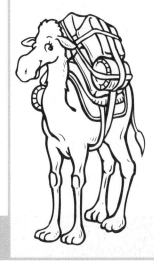

**THURSDAY**                                          **WEEK 26**

Preview the 4 daily lessons to ensure you review or introduce skills that may be unfamiliar to students.

# The International Space Station

side by side, sixteen countries have been working on the International Space Station (ISS) The biggest ~~sceintific~~ scientific project in the history of the world, the iss will be four times as large as the russian Mir space station The iss will be 109 meters (356 ft) across and it'll be 88 meters (290 ft) long. solar panels covering almost a an acre will provide power for lab tests the iss will ~~way~~ weigh over 450,000 kilos (one million lbs)!

| Error Summary | |
|---|---|
| Capitalization | 7 |
| Language Usage | 1 |
| Punctuation: | |
|   Apostrophe | 1 |
|   Comma | 2 |
|   Period | 6 |
| Spelling | 2 |

**MONDAY**      **WEEK 27**

the united states is leading the program but the ISS is truly a International project every country is making a part of the final iss. canada for example is building an Robotic Arm The arm will be 17 meters (55 ft) long and it'll be used to build other parts of the ISS The european space agency for its part is building a lab and transport vehicles. russia moreover is building two research modules ~~module~~. One of the russian modules will transport and transfer crews

| Error Summary | |
|---|---|
| Capitalization | 14 |
| Language Usage | 3 |
| Punctuation: | |
|   Comma | 8 |
|   Period | 5 |

**TUESDAY**      **WEEK 27**

Name _____

# The International Space Station

side by side, sixteen countries have been working on the International Space Station (ISS) The biggest sceintific project in the history of the world the iss will be four times as large as the russian Mir space station The iss will be 109 meters (356 ft) across and itll be 88 meters (290 ft) long. solar panels covering almost a acre will provide power for lab tests the iss will way over 450,000 kilos (one million lbs)!

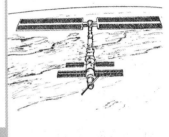

**WATCH FOR**

- names of nationalities
- abbreviations
- acronyms

**MONDAY**                                    **WEEK 27**

---

the united states is leading the program but the ISS is truly a International project every country is making a part of the final iss. canada for example is building an Robotic Arm The arm will be 17 meters (55 ft) long and it'll be used to build other parts of the ISS The european space agency for its part is building a lab and transport vehicles. russia moreover is building two research module. One of the russian modules will transport and transfer crews

**WATCH FOR**

- names of nations
- names of nationalities
- abbreviations
- acronyms

**TUESDAY**                                   **WEEK 27**

ISSs orbit will provide ~~sceintists~~ scientists with a big view of Earth Theyll be able to see 85% of the globes surface, and ~~he ll~~ they'll be able to see 95% of the worlds population this big view, to be sure, will allow ~~scientist~~ scientists to study earths ~~whether~~ weather. The iss, a unique science lab, will allow scientists to study, do experiments, and grow things. Without earths gravity, the results may differ from experiments done on earth. by comparing results, scientists may make new ~~discoverys~~ discoveries about how things work.

| Error Summary | |
|---|---|
| Capitalization | 6 |
| Language Usage | 2 |
| Punctuation: | |
| Apostrophe | 6 |
| Comma | 9 |
| Period | 3 |
| Spelling | 3 |

**WEDNESDAY**                                    **WEEK 27**

the iss, a science space station, makes some people want ~~an~~ a space hotel. a room would be very expensive, but there are millionaires, rock stars, and others who would pay for it. ~~Their~~ There are a few space ~~tourist~~ tourists, in fact, who have already flown into space. they ~~pass~~ passed medical tests, and they paid a lot of money. Worried that tourists will take away from ~~sceince~~ science, some people ~~is~~ are not happy about space tourists. despite their objections, space vacations may not be that far off.

| Error Summary | |
|---|---|
| Capitalization | 5 |
| Language Usage | 4 |
| Punctuation: | |
| Comma | 9 |
| Period | 3 |
| Spelling | 2 |

**THURSDAY**                                     **WEEK 27**

Name _____

ISSs orbit will provide sceintists with a big view of Earth Theyll be able to see 85% of the globes surface and he'll be able to see 95% of the worlds population this big view to be sure will allow scientist to study earths whether. The iss a unique science lab will allow scientists to study do experiments and grow things. Without earths gravity the results may differ from experiments done on earth. by comparing results scientists may make new discoverys about how things work

WATCH FOR
• names of places
• acronyms
• commas

**WEDNESDAY**                                    **WEEK 27**

the iss, a science space station makes some people want an space hotel. a room would be very expensive but there are millionaires rock stars and others who would pay for it Their are a few space tourist in fact who have already flown into space. they pass medical tests and they paid a lot of money Worried that tourists will take away from sceince some people is not happy about space tourists. despite their objections space vacations may not be that far off

WATCH FOR
• acronyms
• commas

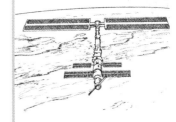

**THURSDAY**                                    **WEEK 27**

Preview the 4 daily lessons to ensure you review or introduce skills that may be unfamiliar to students.

# The Book of Three

In lloyd Alexander's the book of three, the unlikely hero is Taran, an assistant pig-keeper. The Book of Three is a magical ~~tail~~ tale of good and evil set in the mystical land of Prydain taran helps take care of Hen Wen, a visionary talking Pig. Hen Wen doesn't talk to Taran though she only talks to Dallben the magician. The adventures in the book of three begin when Hen Wen runs off into the forest and Taran heads after her.

| Error Summary | |
|---|---|
| Capitalization | 10 |
| Punctuation: | |
| Apostrophe | 2 |
| Comma | 2 |
| Period | 2 |
| Other | 1 |
| Spelling | 1 |

**MONDAY**     **WEEK 28**

Taran's search for Hen Wen takes him on a lively daring ~~journie~~ journey. it is filled with adventure, danger, and strange creatures. Chased by the evil horned king, Taran is saved by the good lord gwydion. Both lord gwydion and the Horned King are seeking hen wen, the pig In the chapter entitled "Gurgi," Taran meets Gurgi, a tangled, furry creature who speaks of "crunchings and munchings." Taran meets a dwarf who wishes to be invisible, and Taran meets a bard whose Harp strings break whenever he "readjusts the facts."

| Error Summary | |
|---|---|
| Capitalization | 10 |
| Punctuation: | |
| Apostrophe | 1 |
| Comma | 9 |
| Period | 2 |
| Quotation Mark | 3 |
| Spelling | 1 |

**TUESDAY**     **WEEK 28**

Name _____

# The Book of Three

In lloyd Alexanders <u>the book of three</u>, the unlikely hero is Taran an assistant pig-keeper. The Book of Three is a magical tail of good and evil set in the mystical land of Prydain taran helps take care of Hen Wen, a visionary talking Pig. Hen Wen doesnt talk to Taran though she only talks to Dallben the magician. The adventures in <u>the book of three</u> begin when Hen Wen runs off into the forest and Taran heads after her.

**WATCH FOR**
- names of people
- titles of books

**MONDAY**          **WEEK 28**

---

Tarans search for Hen Wen takes him on a lively daring journie. it is filled with adventure danger and strange creatures. Chased by the evil horned king. Taran is saved by the good lord gwydion. Both lord gwydion and the Horned King are seeking hen wen the pig In the chapter entitled Gurgi Taran meets Gurgi a tangled furry creature who speaks of "crunchings and munchings." Taran meets a dwarf who wishes to be invisible and Taran meets a bard whose Harp strings break whenever he "readjusts the facts

**WATCH FOR**
- names & titles of people
- names of characters
- titles of chapters
- quotes

**TUESDAY**          **WEEK 28**

Taran's dearest companion in <u>The Book of Three</u> is Eilonwy a girl Taran's age. eilonwy rescues Taran from a dark, dank dungeon after her Aunt an evil sorceress, captures him. Eilonwy does not think Taran is very smart at first And she asks Taran is assistant pig-keeper the kind of work that calls for a great deal of intelligence?" In the chapter entitled the barrow Taran tells Eilonwy that he knew they would get lost. I didn't say i was lost Eilonwy protests. "I only said I didn't know where I was"

### Error Summary

| | |
|---|---|
| Capitalization | 7 |
| **Punctuation:** | |
| Apostrophe | 3 |
| Comma | 8 |
| Period | 1 |
| Quotation Mark | 5 |
| Other | 1 |

**WEDNESDAY**                    **WEEK 28**

---

taran and his companions find Hen Wen at long last and with Hen's Wen's help, the horned king is defeated. In the final chapter, entitled Welcomes, Taran is asked what he thinks about being a hero. Taran responds what i mostly did was make mistakes" It is Taran's mistakes, though, that make <u>the book of three</u> such a enchanting tail even when Taran does make a mistake he never gives up. He keep to his quest and it is his efforts that keep his companions together.

*an* (above "a")
*tale* (above "tail")
*keeps* (above "keep")
*together* (above "togeather")

### Error Summary

| | |
|---|---|
| Capitalization | 7 |
| Language Usage | 2 |
| **Punctuation:** | |
| Apostrophe | 1 |
| Comma | 5 |
| Period | 2 |
| Quotation Mark | 3 |
| Other | 1 |
| Spelling | 3 |

**THURSDAY**                    **WEEK 28**

Name _____

Tarans dearest companion in The Book of Three is Eilonwy a girl Tarans age. eilonwy rescues Taran from a dark dank dungeon after her Aunt an evil sorceress captures him. Eilonwy does not think Taran is very smart at first And she asks Taran is assistant pig-keeper the kind of work that calls for a great deal of intelligence?" In the chapter entitled the barrow Taran tells Eilonwy that he knew they would get lost. I didnt say i was lost Eilonwy protests. "I only said I didn't know where I was"

- titles of books
- titles of chapters
- names of people
- quotes

**WEDNESDAY**                                    **WEEK 28**

taran and his companions find Hen Wen at long last and with Hen's Wen's help, the horned king is defeated. In the final chapter, entitled Welcomes, Taran is asked what he thinks about being a hero. Taran responds what i mostly did was make mistakes" It is Tarans mistakes though, that make the book of three such a enchanting tail even when Taran does make a mistake. he never gives up. He keep to his quest and it is his efforts that keep his companions togeather.

- titles of books
- titles of chapters
- quotes

**THURSDAY**                                      **WEEK 28**

Preview the 4 daily lessons to ensure you review or introduce skills that may be unfamiliar to students.

# The United States Court System

the purpose of the court system in the united
states is to protect every citizen. ~~Their~~ There are two
levels of courts in the United States these are state
and federal. cases go to the state courts when state
laws ~~is~~ are broken they go to the federal courts when
federal laws are ~~broke~~ broken State courts ~~handel~~ handle crimes
that fall under state law while, on the other hand,
federal courts deal with crimes involving violations of
the u.s. constitution, federal laws, and disputes involving
citizens from other nations.

| Error Summary | |
|---|---|
| Capitalization | 8 |
| Language Usage | 2 |
| Punctuation: | |
| Comma | 3 |
| Period | 4 |
| Spelling | 2 |

**MONDAY**                                **WEEK 29**

Neither state nor federal courts ~~makes~~ make laws.
they only interpret and apply them This means
that a judge ~~canot~~ cannot make laws. A judge has to
follow specific rules that regulate our court system.
Within the US. court system, ~~their is~~ there are two types of
trials. one is civil; one is criminal. In civil ~~trails~~ trials,
disputes are settled between the plaintiff and the
defendant In criminal trials, on the other hand, the
government attorney, or prosecutor, makes a case
against the defendant.

| Error Summary | |
|---|---|
| Capitalization | 2 |
| Language Usage | 2 |
| Punctuation: | |
| Comma | 4 |
| Period | 4 |
| Spelling | 3 |

**TUESDAY**                                **WEEK 29**

Name _____

# The United States Court System

the purpose of the court system in the united states is to protect every citizen. Their are two levels of courts in the United States these are state and federal. cases go to the state courts when state laws is broken they go to the federal courts when federal laws are broke State courts handel crimes that fall under state law while on the other hand federal courts deal with crimes involving violations of the u.s. constitution, federal laws and disputes involving citizens from other nations

 WATCH FOR

- names of countries
- abbreviations of countries

**MONDAY**                                         **WEEK 29**

Neither state nor federal courts makes laws. they only interpret and apply them This means that a judge canot make laws. A judge has to follow specific rules that regulate our court system. Within the US. court system their is two types of trials. one is civil; one is criminal. In civil trails, disputes are settled between the plaintiff and the defendant In criminal trials on the other hand the government attorney, or prosecutor makes a case against the defendant

WATCH FOR

- abbreviations

**TUESDAY**                                         **WEEK 29**

In both civil and criminal cases, a trial may be appealed if a lawyer feels that a judge's ruling did not follow the rules. When this happens, the case goes ~~go~~ to the court ~~cort~~ of appeals. In this type of court, there is no jury because the court is not deciding guilt. The Court of Appeals is ~~are~~ made up of a panel of judges. These judges decide whether ~~wheather~~ the judge in the trial case followed the rules if a person is dissatisfied ~~disatisfied~~ with the court of appeals's ruling, he or she may then appeal at the final U.S. supreme court level.

### Error Summary

| | |
|---|---|
| Capitalization | 5 |
| Language Usage | 2 |
| Punctuation: | |
|   Apostrophe | 1 |
|   Comma | 3 |
|   Period | 2 |
| Spelling | 4 |

**WEDNESDAY**                    **WEEK 29**

There is both a federal and a state supreme court. The US Supreme Court, the court at the federal level, is the highest court in the country. All the supreme court justices choose which ~~witch~~ cases they will hear. Around 5,000 cases are ~~is~~ given to the u.s. supreme court each year, and they typically hear ~~here~~ only 100 to 125 of them. The US supreme court is the only court that can strike down state or federal laws. only a future U.S. supreme court can, in fact, overturn a U.S. supreme court ruling.

### Error Summary

| | |
|---|---|
| Capitalization | 15 |
| Language Usage | 1 |
| Punctuation: | |
|   Comma | 4 |
|   Period | 8 |
| Spelling | 2 |

**THURSDAY**                    **WEEK 29**

Name _____

In both civil and criminal cases a trial may be appealed if a lawyer feels that a judges ruling did not follow the rules. When this happens, the case go to the cort of appeals. In this type of court there is no jury because the court is not deciding guilt. The Court of Appeals are made up of a panel of judges. These judges decide wheather the judge in the trial case followed the rules if a person is disatisfied with the court of appeals's ruling he or she may then appeal at the final U.S. supreme court level

**WATCH FOR**

• names of institutions

| **WEDNESDAY** | **WEEK 29** |
|---|---|

There is both a federal and a state supreme court The US Supreme Court, the court at the federal level is the Highest Court in the country. All the supreme court justices choose witch cases they will hear. Around 5,000 cases is given to the u.s supreme court each year and they typically here only 100 to 125 of them. The US supreme court is the only court that can strike down state or federal laws only a future U.S. supreme court can in fact overturn a U.S. supreme court ruling

**WATCH FOR**

• abbreviations of country names

• names of institutions

| **THURSDAY** | **WEEK 29** |
|---|---|

Preview the 4 daily lessons to ensure you review or introduce skills that may be unfamiliar to students.

# Coed Competitive Sports

There are those who argue for coed competitive sports. They feel that everyone should compete on an equal basis so they push for teams of boys and girls. Rather than saying "let the best man win," they say let the best player win These people feel they are helping students by creating a system of true competition i on the other hand disagree? I feel that coed competitive sports may not be in the best interest of students sports or competition

**MONDAY**      **WEEK 30**

| Error Summary | |
| --- | --- |
| Capitalization | 3 |
| Language Usage | 4 |
| Punctuation: | |
| Comma | 8 |
| Period | 4 |
| Quotation Mark | 2 |
| Spelling | 1 |

It might be fine to say "let the best player win" when talking about professional sports but that doesn't apply at the school level? schools are for education, Not for producing professional athletes. While in school students need to learn the importance of fitness exercise and staying in shape If the focus is "winner take all" too many students will be left out of sports boys and girls who may have their growth spurts later, or are smaller in build, will not be included. this sends students the wrong message about fitness and health

**TUESDAY**      **WEEK 30**

| Error Summary | |
| --- | --- |
| Capitalization | 5 |
| Language Usage | 3 |
| Punctuation: | |
| Apostrophe | 1 |
| Comma | 7 |
| Period | 4 |
| Quotation Mark | 2 |
| Spelling | 1 |

Name _____

# Coed Competitive Sports

- quotes
- commas

Their are those whom argue for coed competitive sports. They feel that everyone should compete on a equal basis so they push for teams of boys and girl. Rather than saying "let the best man win." they say let the best player win These people feel they is helping students by creating a system of true competition i on the other hand disagree? I feel that coed competitive sports may not be in the best interest of students sports or competition

**MONDAY**　　　　　　　　　　　　　　　　　　**WEEK 30**

It might be fine to say let the best player win" when talking about professional sports but that doesnt apply at the school level? schools are for education, Not for producing professional athletes. While in school students need to learn the importance of fitness exercise and staying in shape If the focus is winner take all" too many students will be left out of sports boys and girl whom may have their growth spurts later, or is smaller in build, will not be included. this sends students the wrong mesage about fitness and health

- quotes
- commas

**TUESDAY**　　　　　　　　　　　　　　　　　　**WEEK 30**

There is a song entitled "let it be" and that is
what many schools want to do with they're sports
their
programs change however is necessary. rather than
allow the system to let it be," we must create equal
believe
opportunity. i beleive resources should be shared fairly
between boys and girls. When gym use, uniforms and
coaching staff for example are all equally shared
is
schools will be showing that physical activity are
important for every student, boy or girl.

**Error Summary**

| | |
|---|---|
| Capitalization | 6 |
| Language Usage | 1 |
| Punctuation: | |
| Comma | 8 |
| Period | 2 |
| Quotation Mark | 2 |
| Spelling | 2 |

**WEDNESDAY                    WEEK 30**

believe                                    is
i beleive however that there are no such thing
as a "boy" sport or a "girl" sport in cases where there
is only a boys cross-country track team, for example
girls should be allowed to join until theres a team of
their own. when it comes to cheerleading an activity
boys
now considered a sport, both boy and girls should
be allowed to participate. if a school does have
an
cheerleaders, they should attend a equal number of
boys and girls sporting events These are all steps
toward making school sports more fair.

**Error Summary**

| | |
|---|---|
| Capitalization | 4 |
| Language Usage | 3 |
| Punctuation: | |
| Apostrophe | 4 |
| Comma | 6 |
| Period | 2 |
| Quotation Mark | 2 |
| Spelling | 1 |

**THURSDAY                    WEEK 30**

Name _____

There is a song entitled "let it be and that is what many schools want to do with they're sports programs change however is necessary. rather than allow the system to let it be." we must create equal opportunity. i beleive resources should be shared fairly between boys and girls. When gym use, uniforms and coaching staff for example are all equally shared schools will be showing that physical activity are important for every student, boy or girl

**WATCH FOR**

• song titles
• quotes
• commas

---

**WEDNESDAY**                                    **WEEK 30**

---

i beleive however that there are no such thing as a "boy" sport or a girl sport in cases where there is only a boys cross-country track team for example girls should be allowed to join until theres a team of their own. when it comes to cheerleading an activity now considered a sport, both boy and girls should be allowed to participate. if a school does have cheerleaders they should attend a equal number of boys and girls sporting events These are all steps toward making school sports more fair.

**WATCH FOR**

• special words in quotes
• commas

---

**THURSDAY**                                     **WEEK 30**

Preview the 4 daily lessons to ensure you review or introduce skills that may be unfamiliar to students.

# Bird-Watching in Australia

We ~~we're~~ *were* the only ones on the trail, and at first I could not understand why? I am a bird watcher and I had made my family come with ~~I~~ *me* to a park in Queensland, australia. we were looking for the purple-breasted fruit dove, a purple and yellow bird. it was warm in the dark, wet rainforest, and we were wearing shorts. "everyone, this is wonderful," I said. I dont understand why were the only ones here." That was when i noticed the mud on our legs.

### Error Summary

| | |
|---|---|
| Capitalization | 8 |
| Language Usage | 1 |
| Punctuation: | |
|   Apostrophe | 2 |
|   Comma | 8 |
|   Period | 3 |
|   Quotation Mark | 1 |
| Spelling | 1 |

**MONDAY**      **WEEK 31**

---

While birding at another park, a woman had warned ~~we~~ *us* about leeches. "my dears, they crawl across rocks and over the ground. They will squeeze into the shoelace holes of your shoes," she said. we nodded politely, but we didnt believe her. How could leeches move across the ground? She just wanted to scare us with a tall, creepy ~~tail~~ *tale*. We found out she was telling the truth. The leeches are little, but they can sense heat. With unbelievable quickness, they can inch to it's source.

### Error Summary

| | |
|---|---|
| Capitalization | 3 |
| Language Usage | 1 |
| Punctuation: | |
|   Apostrophe | 2 |
|   Comma | 7 |
|   Period | 1 |
|   Other | 1 |
| Spelling | 1 |

**TUESDAY**      **WEEK 31**

Name _____

# Bird-Watching in Australia

We we're the only ones on the trail and at first I could not understand why? I am a bird watcher and I had made my family come with I to a park in Queensland australia. we were looking for the purple-breasted Fruit Dove. A purple and yellow bird. it was warm in the dark wet rainforest and we were wearing shorts. "everyone this is wonderful" I said. I dont understand why were the only ones here" That was when i noticed the mud on our legs

WATCH FOR
- commas
- quotes

**MONDAY**                                    **WEEK 31**

---

While birding at another park. A woman had warned we about leeches. "my dears they crawl across rocks and over the ground. They will squeeze into the shoelace holes of your shoes" she said. we nodded politely but we didnt believe her. How could leeches move across the ground. She just wanted to scare us with a tall creepy tail. We found out she was telling the truth. The leeches are little but they can sense heat. With unbelievable quickness they can inch to it's source

WATCH FOR
- commas
- quotes
- question marks

**TUESDAY**                                    **WEEK 31**

<u>m</u>y children were delighted with the leeches and they laughed in wonder. <u>t</u>hey started a competition. Who could stretch a <u>l</u>eech the farthest before ~~he~~ <sup>it</sup> ~~finally~~ came off? Putting one on each finger my oldest son danced around and said "hey mom want to shake?" My youngest boy ~~actualy~~ <sup>actually</sup> began to cry because the leeches weren't interested in him! He wasn't as "hot" as the two older children Unlike my children I wasn't happy I was scared horrified and miserable. As <u>i</u> saw a leech slip into my shoelace hole I ran.

**Error Summary**

| | |
|---|---|
| Capitalization | 5 |
| Language Usage | 1 |
| Punctuation: | |
|    Apostrophe | 3 |
|    Comma | 9 |
|    Period | 2 |
|    Quotation Mark | 1 |
|    Other | 2 |
| Spelling | 2 |

**WEDNESDAY**                                        **WEEK 31**

All of a sudden the call of the purple-breasted <u>f</u>ruit <u>d</u>ove made its way across the forest. <u>h</u>igh on a branch the bird sat majestically in it's royal colors. "<u>m</u>om why don't you look at the bird longer?" my children asked. "<u>y</u>ou made us come here instead of the beach. Now mom don't you think you need to stay really still and look at ~~her~~ <sup>it</sup> longer?" I couldn't because all <u>i</u> could think about was what was crawling into my shoe Need I mention that our next stop was the beach?

**Error Summary**

| | |
|---|---|
| Capitalization | 7 |
| Language Usage | 1 |
| Punctuation: | |
|    Apostrophe | 4 |
|    Comma | 5 |
|    Period | 1 |
|    Quotation Mark | 1 |
|    Other | 3 |

**THURSDAY**                                         **WEEK 31**

Name _____

my children were delighted with the leeches and they laughed in wonder. they started a competition. Who could stretch a leech the farthest before he finaly came off. Putting one on each finger my oldest son danced around and said "hey mom want to shake" My youngest boy actualy began to cry because the leeches werent interested in him! He wasnt as "hot as the two older children Unlike my children I wasnt happy I was scared horrified and miserable. As i saw a leech slip into my shoelace hole I ran.

WATCH FOR

- commas
- question marks
- special words in quotes

**WEDNESDAY**                                    **WEEK 31**

All of a sudden the call of the purple-breasted Fruit Dove made its way across the forest. high on a branch the bird sat majestically in it's royal colors. "mom why dont you look at the bird longer my children asked. "you made us come here instead of the beach. Now mom dont you think you need to stay really still and look at her longer" I couldnt because all i could think about was what was crawling into my shoe Need I mention that our next stop was the beach

WATCH FOR

- commas
- quotes
- question marks

**THURSDAY**                                    **WEEK 31**

Preview the 4 daily lessons to ensure you review or introduce skills that may be unfamiliar to students.

# Talking About Time

"Dr Spark, is it true you want to change the way we tell time?"

Yes, Mr Forest i think we need to make some changes"

dr. spark I dont think its ~~possable~~ possible to change time

"time of course cant be changed Mr forest, but we can be consistent about our description of time

What in the world do you mean dr spark?"

I mean Mr Forest that we need to switch to a 24-hour clock

| Error Summary | |
| --- | --- |
| Capitalization | 7 |
| Punctuation: | |
| Apostrophe | 3 |
| Comma | 8 |
| Period | 9 |
| Quotation Mark | 7 |
| Other | 2 |
| Spelling | 1 |

**MONDAY**          **WEEK 32**

dr spark what do you mean by a 24-hour clock?"

A 24-hour clock Mr Forest does not use am and pm

"then how would we know if it was 100 a.m. or 1:00 p.m. Dr. Spark?"

There
"~~Their~~ is no mistaking the hour with a 24-hour clock. You see mr. Forest, 100 Am is simply written as 1:00, but 100 pM becomes 1300

does this mean dr spark, that 200 pm would be 14:00, 300 p.m would be 1500 and 1100 P.M. would be 23:00?

believe
mr Forest i ~~beleive~~ you now see how a 24-hour clock works.

| Error Summary | |
| --- | --- |
| Capitalization | 13 |
| Punctuation: | |
| Comma | 8 |
| Period | 16 |
| Quotation Mark | 10 |
| Other | 14 |
| Spelling | 2 |

**TUESDAY**          **WEEK 32**

Name _____

# Talking About Time

"Dr Spark, is it true you want to change the way we tell time"

Yes, Mr Forest i think we need to make some changes"

dr. spark I dont think its possable to change time

"time of course cant be changed Mr forest, but we can be consistent about our description of time

What in the world do you mean dr spark"

I mean Mr Forest that we need to switch to a 24-hour clock

| MONDAY | WEEK 32 |
|---|---|

dr spark what do you mean by a 24-hour clock

A 24 hour clock Mr Forest does not use am and pm

"then how would we know if it was 100 a.m. or 1:00 p.m. Dr. Spark

"Their is no mistaking the hour with a 24 hour clock. You see mr. Forest, 100 Am is simply written as 1:00, but 100 pM becomes 1300

does this mean dr spark, that 200 pm would be 14:00, 300 p.m would be 1500 and 1100 P.M. would be 23:00

mr Forest i beleive you now see how a 24 hour clock works.

| TUESDAY | WEEK 32 |
|---|---|

"Dr Spark isn't it ~~to~~ too confusing to change to a 24-hour clock?"

"on the contrary mr forest a 24-hour clock is practical easy and consistent"

Then why isn't it being used now dr spark?

Actually, Mr Forest the military and some countries, like denmark, are ~~all ready~~ already using it

dr Spark why is that?"

"There ~~are~~ is less room for error mr forest

**Error Summary**

| | |
|---|---|
| Capitalization | 9 |
| Language Usage | 1 |
| Punctuation: | |
| Apostrophe | 2 |
| Comma | 9 |
| Period | 9 |
| Quotation Mark | 6 |
| Other | 4 |
| Spelling | 2 |

---

**WEDNESDAY**      **WEEK 32**

---

"why Dr Spark ~~their~~ there is little room for error now. When it's light and day it's AM. when it's dark and night, it's pm

"What if you live where the sun never sets mr. Forest?

"That's right! days are shorter or longer, depending on the time of the year

actually Mr Forest the hours of daylight may change but days aren't longer or shorter. There ~~is~~ are always 24 hours in a day

well dr spark it certainly would make setting my alarm clock easier"

**Error Summary**

| | |
|---|---|
| Capitalization | 10 |
| Language Usage | 1 |
| Punctuation: | |
| Apostrophe | 4 |
| Comma | 9 |
| Period | 9 |
| Quotation Mark | 7 |
| Spelling | 1 |

---

Name _____

"Dr Spark isnt it to confusing to change to a 24 hour clock"

"on the contrary mr forest a 24-hour clock is practical easy and consistent"

Then why isnt it being used now dr spark

Actually, Mr Forest the military and some countries, like denmark, are all ready using it

dr Spark why is that"

"There are less room for error mr forest

**WATCH FOR**

- dialog
- question marks
- hyphens
- commas

| WEDNESDAY | WEEK 32 |

"why Dr Spark their is little room for error now. When it's light and day its AM. when its dark and night, it's pm

"What if you live where the sun never sets mr. Forest?

"Thats right! days are shorter or longer, depending on the time of the year

actually Mr Forest the hours of daylight may change but days arent longer or shorter. There is always 24 hours in a day

well dr spark it certainly would make setting my alarm clock easier

**WATCH FOR**

- dialog
- abbreviations
- commas

| THURSDAY | WEEK 32 |

Preview the 4 daily lessons to ensure you review or introduce skills that may be unfamiliar to students.

# Apollo 13

On april 13, 1970, astronaut James Lovell and his crew ~~was~~ were on their way to the moon. Fifty-six hours into the mission, the No. 2 oxygen tank exploded, causing ~~grate~~ great damage to the Odyssey, their spaceship. "Houston, we've had a problem," Lovell told Mission Control. lovell and his men were 200,000 miles from Earth, floating through space without any assurance that ~~he~~ they would ever return.

| Error Summary | |
|---|---|
| **Capitalization** | 2 |
| **Language Usage** | 2 |
| **Punctuation:** | |
| Apostrophe | 1 |
| Comma | 4 |
| Period | 1 |
| Quotation Mark | 1 |
| Other | 2 |
| **Spelling** | 1 |

**MONDAY**　　　　　　　　　　　　　　　　**WEEK 33**

---

~~Imediately~~ Immediately after the explosion, lovell reported seeing some type of gas leaking from the ship. it was oxygen! the astronauts had to abandon ship and seek refuge in the Aquarius, the lunar module. The Aquarius ~~is~~ was not made to support three men; it had been designed to land on the moon. As the astronauts did their best to conserve power, heat, and water, Mission control had to come up with an immediate plan to keep the men from ~~dicing~~ dying of dangerous carbon dioxide poisoning.

| Error Summary | |
|---|---|
| **Capitalization** | 4 |
| **Language Usage** | 1 |
| **Punctuation:** | |
| Comma | 3 |
| Period | 2 |
| Other | 2 |
| **Spelling** | 2 |

**TUESDAY**　　　　　　　　　　　　　　　**WEEK 33**

Name _____

# Apollo 13

On april 13 1970, astronaut James Lovell and his crew was on their way to the moon. Fifty six hours into the mission the No. 2 oxygen tank exploded, causing grate damage to the Odyssey their spaceship. "Houston weve had a problem, Lovell told Mission Control. lovell and his men were 200,000 miles from Earth, floating through space without any assurance that he would ever return

- hyphens
- names of spacecraft
- quotes

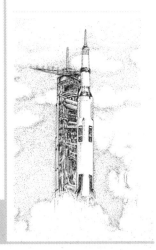

| **MONDAY** | **WEEK 33** |
|---|---|

Imediately after the explosion lovell reported seeing some type of gas leaking from the ship it was oxygen! the astronauts had to abandon ship and seek refuge in the <u>Aquarius</u>, the lunar module. The Aquarius is not made to support three men it had been designed to land on the moon. As the astronauts did their best to conserve power heat, and water Mission control had to come up with an immediate plan to keep the men from dieing of dangerous carbon dioxide poisoning?

- names of spacecraft
- semicolons

| **TUESDAY** | **WEEK 33** |
|---|---|

A special filter was ~~quick~~ quickly designed to save the men. Only materials that the astronauts had on hand could be used. Plastic bags, cardboard boxes, and tape were used. Apollo 13's mission had changed, going to the moon was no longer the mission's objective. The goal was to get the cold, hungry, and thirsty astronauts home alive. As Mission Control worked on a solution, people all over the world waited and watched. ~~Wood~~ Would the crew be saved and the mission declared a "successful failure"?

**Error Summary**

| Language Usage | 1 |
|---|---|
| Punctuation: | |
| Apostrophe | 2 |
| Comma | 5 |
| Other | 2 |
| Spelling | 1 |

**WEDNESDAY**                    **WEEK 33**

The crew was able ~~too~~ to determine its position by using the sun as a guide. The astronauts burst back into earth's atmosphere, landing safely in the south pacific. Tests on the spaceship later showed that the No. 2 oxygen tank on the Odyssey had been faulty. It had failed tests before and had even been removed from Apollo 10! The Astronauts and Mission Control avoided a complete disaster by working together. The men had survived, the mission was declared a "successful failure."

**Error Summary**

| Capitalization | 5 |
|---|---|
| Punctuation: | |
| Apostrophe | 1 |
| Period | 2 |
| Quotation Mark | 1 |
| Other | 2 |
| Spelling | 1 |

**THURSDAY**                    **WEEK 33**

Name _____

A special filter was quick designed to save the men. Only materials that the astronauts had on hand could be used. Plastic bags cardboard boxes and tape were used. Apollo 13s mission had changed going to the moon was no longer the missions objective. The goal was to get the cold hungry and thirsty astronauts home alive. As Mission Control worked on a solution people all over the world waited and watched. Wood the crew be saved and the mission declared a "successful failure"

WATCH FOR

- semicolons
- special words in quotes
- question marks

**WEDNESDAY**                                    **WEEK 33**

The crew was able too determine its position by using the sun as a guide. The astronauts burst back into earths atmosphere, landing safely in the south pacific. Tests on the spaceship later showed that the No. 2 oxygen tank on the Odyssey had been faulty it had failed tests before and had even been removed from Apollo 10! The Astronauts and Mission Control avoided a complete disaster by working together. The men had survived the mission was declared a successful failure"

WATCH FOR

- names of spacecraft
- semicolons
- special words in quotes

**THURSDAY**                                    **WEEK 33**

Preview the 4 daily lessons to ensure you review or introduce skills that may be unfamiliar to students.

# Marco Polo's Tales

marco polo our neighbor returned last week from asia Its 1295, and Marco has been away for 24 years He is telling everyone storys *stories* about gold silver and riches but my parents neighbors and friends dont *believe* beleive him. How can there be a palace with a dining hall big enough to seat 6,000 people? my Mother asked me. she said i think marco is just telling crazy imaginative tales about a man he calls Kublai Khan

**Error Summary**

| | |
|---|---|
| Capitalization | 7 |
| Punctuation: | |
| Apostrophe | 2 |
| Comma | 9 |
| Period | 3 |
| Quotation Mark | 4 |
| Spelling | 2 |

**MONDAY**      **WEEK 34**

---

marco our neighbor whom *who* just returned from asia says that the chinese have paper money. Instead of paying with gold silver and goods people can pay with paper The paper is special and its worth a certain amount of gold. Wow! That sure would make buying selling and trading easyer" *easier* I said. Instead of carrying around heavy bulky gold you can just carry paper" my parent's nieghbors *neighbors* and friends is *are* tired of Marcos tales But i could listen to his colorful wild stories all day

**Error Summary**

| | |
|---|---|
| Capitalization | 6 |
| Language Usage | 2 |
| Punctuation: | |
| Apostrophe | 2 |
| Comma | 15 |
| Period | 3 |
| Quotation Mark | 2 |
| Other | 1 |
| Spelling | 3 |

**TUESDAY**      **WEEK 34**

EMC 2729 • Daily Paragraph Editing, Grade 6 • ©2004 by Evan-Moor Corp.

Name _____

# Marco Polo's Tales

marco polo our neighbor returned last week from asia Its 1295, and Marco has been away for 24 years He is telling everyone storys about gold silver and riches but my parents neighbors and friends dont beleive him. How can there be a palace with a dining hall big enough to seat 6,000 people? my Mother asked me. she said i think marco is just telling crazy imaginative tales about a man he calls Kublai Khan

**MONDAY**        **WEEK 34**

marco our neighbor whom just returned from asia says that the chinese have paper money. Instead of paying with gold silver and goods people can pay with paper The paper is special and its worth a certain amount of gold. Wow That sure would make buying selling and trading easyer" I said. Instead of carrying around heavy bulky gold you can just carry paper" my parent's nieghbors and friends is tired of Marcos tales. But i could listen to his colorful wild stories all day

**TUESDAY**        **WEEK 34**

I said wow! when marco our neighbor told ~~myself~~ me
about the chinese postal system He said that china
has three classes of mail. They are first, second, and
priority. Swift, young foot-runners carry second-class
mail between stations that are three ~~mile~~ miles apart. That
way, a ten-day journey can be completed in 24 hours.
Horses ~~is~~ are used to carry the first-class mail, but the
priority mail is the most amazing. only the imperial
majesty uses priority mail, and that mail can be
~~carryed~~ carried 250 to 300 miles a day.

**Error Summary**

| | |
|---|---|
| Capitalization | 7 |
| Language Usage | 3 |
| Punctuation: | |
|   Comma | 8 |
|   Period | 4 |
|   Quotation Mark | 2 |
|   Other | 4 |
| Spelling | 1 |

**WEDNESDAY**      **WEEK 34**

"Wow! I said how is that possible? Marco told
me that only the fastest horses are used. the riders
have a special horn, and they blow it when they get
close to the next station When the new rider and
his horse hear it, they get ready marco, the traveler
also told me about a great canal system, paperback
books, and stones called "coal" that burn like logs.
My parents, friends, and ~~nieghbors~~ neighbors dont believe
Marcos wild, amazing stories about his 24-year
adventure, but i do.

**Error Summary**

| | |
|---|---|
| Capitalization | 4 |
| Punctuation: | |
|   Apostrophe | 2 |
|   Comma | 10 |
|   Period | 4 |
|   Quotation Mark | 4 |
|   Other | 3 |
| Spelling | 1 |

**THURSDAY**      **WEEK 34**

     EMC 2729 • Daily Paragraph Editing, Grade 6 • ©2004 by Evan-Moor Corp.

Name _____

I said wow when marco our neighbor told myself about the chinese postal system He said that china has three classes of mail. They are first second and priority. Swift young foot runners carry second-class mail between stations that are three mile apart That way, a ten day journey can be completed in 24 hours Horses is used to carry the first class mail but the priority mail is the most amazing. only the imperial majesty uses priority mail and that mail can be carryed 250 to 300 miles a day

WATCH FOR

- names of places
- names of nationalities
- dialog
- exclamation points

**WEDNESDAY**       **WEEK 34**

"Wow I said how is that possible Marco told me that only the fastest horses are used. the riders have a special horn and they blow it when they get close to the next station When the new rider and his horse hear it they get ready marco the traveler also told me about a great canal system paperback books and stones called coal" that burn like logs. My parents friends and nieghbors dont believe Marcos wild amazing stories about his 24 year adventure but i do

WATCH FOR

- dialog
- exclamation points
- hyphens

**THURSDAY**       **WEEK 34**

Preview the 4 daily lessons to ensure you review or introduce skills that may be unfamiliar to students.

# Madagascar: A Remote Paradise

Madagascar the worlds fourth-largest island is more like a microcontinent. Isolated from the rest of the world for over 60 million years madagascar is located in the indian ocean 250 miles off the eastern coast of africa The island lies just south of the equator and it has a tropical climate. Their are only two seasons: the rainy and the dry. many of the plants and animals in madagascar is not found anywhere else in the world

*(correction: Their → There; is → are)*

**Error Summary**

| | |
|---|---|
| Capitalization | 6 |
| Language Usage | 1 |
| Punctuation: | |
| Apostrophe | 1 |
| Comma | 4 |
| Period | 2 |
| Other | 1 |
| Spelling | 1 |

**MONDAY** — **WEEK 35**

---

Although madagascar is one of the worlds poorest countries its one of the richest when it comes to biodiversity Nine-tenths of the worlds lemurs are found in madagascar. lemurs a type of primate typically have large eyes woolly fur and a long tail. most lemurs live in trees and there are one type that can leap 30 feet or more from branch to branch. The smallest lemur cant leap that far but its no bigger than a mouse the biggest lemur is the size of a large cat

*(correction: are → is)*

**Error Summary**

| | |
|---|---|
| Capitalization | 5 |
| Language Usage | 1 |
| Punctuation: | |
| Apostrophe | 5 |
| Comma | 7 |
| Period | 3 |
| Other | 1 |

**TUESDAY** — **WEEK 35**

Name _____

# Madagascar: A Remote Paradise

Madagascar the worlds fourth largest island is more like a microcontinent. Isolated from the rest of the world for over 60 million years madagascar is located in the indian ocean 250 miles off the eastern coast of africa The island lies just south of the equator and it has a tropical climate. Their are only two seasons: the rainy and the dry. many of the plants and animals in madagascar is not found anywhere else in the world

- names of places
- commas

**MONDAY**                                    **WEEK 35**

Although madagascar is one of the worlds poorest countries its one of the richest when it comes to biodiversity Nine tenths of the worlds lemurs are found in madagascar. lemurs a type of primate typically have large eyes woolly fur and a long tail. most lemurs live in trees and there are one type that can leap 30 feet or more from branch to branch. The smallest lemur cant leap that far but its no bigger than a mouse the biggest lemur is the size of a large cat

- names of places
- commas
- hyphens

**TUESDAY**                                    **WEEK 35**

with it's abundance of microclimates madagascar is home to all types of creatures Over one-half of the worlds varieties of chameleons are found in madagascar Chameleons known for ~~they're~~ their ability to change color, are small lizard-like reptiles that live in trees. Chameleons use their sticky tongues, which measure up to one and one-half times the length of their bodies, to catch insects. a chameleon ~~have~~ has two eyes and each eye can move independently of the other

| Error Summary | |
|---|---|
| Capitalization | 4 |
| Language Usage | 1 |
| Punctuation: | |
| Apostrophe | 2 |
| Comma | 3 |
| Period | 3 |
| Other | 3 |
| Spelling | 1 |

**WEDNESDAY**        **WEEK 35**

With over 10,000 ~~varietys~~ varieties of plants madagascar has some of the richest flora in the world Some trees have bulging trunks where water is stored there ~~are~~ is even one plant that eats meat. Drawn by the smell of nectar insects crawl into the plants "bowl where they are then ~~traped~~ trapped. When something is "endemic" that means that it is found only in a particular place? Of the 150 species of frogs found in madagascar 148 are endemic. so are many of it's orchids birds trees and insects

| Error Summary | |
|---|---|
| Capitalization | 4 |
| Language Usage | 1 |
| Punctuation: | |
| Apostrophe | 2 |
| Comma | 7 |
| Period | 4 |
| Quotation Mark | 2 |
| Spelling | 2 |

**THURSDAY**        **WEEK 35**

EMC 2729 • Daily Paragraph Editing, Grade 6 • ©2004 by Evan-Moor Corp.

Name _____

with it's abundance of microclimates madagascar is home to all types of creatures Over one half of the worlds varieties of chameleons are found in madagascar Chameleons known for they're ability to change color, are small lizard like reptiles that live in trees. Chameleons use their sticky tongues, which measure up to one and one half times the length of their bodies, to catch insects. a chameleon have two eyes and each eye can move independently of the other

WATCH FOR

- names of places
- commas
- hyhens

**WEDNESDAY**                                          **WEEK 35**

With over 10,000 varietys of plants madagascar has some of the richest flora in the world Some trees have bulging trunks where water is stored there are even one plant that eats meat. Drawn by the smell of nectar insects crawl into the plants "bowl where they are then traped. When something is endemic" that means that it is found only in a particular place? Of the 150 species of frogs found in madagascar 148 are endemic. so are many of it's orchids birds trees and insects

WATCH FOR

- names of places
- commas
- special words in quotes

**THURSDAY**                                          **WEEK 35**

Preview the 4 daily lessons to ensure you review or introduce skills that may be unfamiliar to students.

# Dining Directions

You ~~is~~ (are) eating dinner with the company President tonight, and you don't want to make ~~no~~ (any) mistakes. "Oh, how do I know what fork to use?" you ask. "What if I use the wrong bread plate?" You want to make a good impression, so you ~~reveiw~~ (review) proper dining directions. The first rule you remember is "outside in, there may be three spoons, but the one you use first is on the outside, farthest away from the plate. Silverware is used outside in.

| Error Summary | |
|---|---|
| Capitalization | 2 |
| Language Usage | 2 |
| Punctuation: | |
| Comma | 4 |
| Period | 1 |
| Quotation Mark | 3 |
| Other | 1 |
| Spelling | 1 |

**MONDAY**　　　　　　　　**WEEK 36**

Thinking of rules, water glasses, bread plates, and what belongs to whom, you remember the words "lefty lumpy, righty runny." Lumpy foods, or solids, are on the left; runny foods, or liquids, are on the right. Your bread plate will be on the left because bread is a solid; your water glass will be on the right because water, of course, is a liquid. "I won't use ~~no~~ (the) wrong glass now," you say confidently to yourself. With proper etiquette, you (will) be sure to make a good ~~impresion~~ (impression).

| Error Summary | |
|---|---|
| Language Usage | 2 |
| Punctuation: | |
| Comma | 5 |
| Quotation Mark | 1 |
| Other | 1 |
| Spelling | 1 |

**TUESDAY**　　　　　　　　**WEEK 36**

Name _____

# Dining Directions

You is eating dinner with the company President tonight and you don't want to make no mistakes. "Oh how do I know what fork to use? you ask. What if I use the wrong bread plate" You want to make a good impression so you reveiw proper dining directions. The first rule you remember is "outside in there may be three spoons but the one you use first is on the outside, farthest away from the plate. Silverware is used outside in.

- quotes
- special words in quotes
- question marks

**MONDAY**                                                    **WEEK 36**

Thinking of rules, water glasses bread plates, and what belongs to whom you remember the words "lefty lumpy, righty runny. Lumpy foods, or solids, are on the left; runny foods, or liquids are on the right. Your bread plate will be on the left because bread is a solid your water glass will be on the right because water of course is a liquid. "I won't use no wrong glass now," you say confidently to yourself. With proper etiquette, you be sure to make a good impresion.

- special words in quotes
- semicolons

**TUESDAY**                                                    **WEEK 36**

The phrase "As I send my ship to sea, I sip my soup away from me" helps you remember proper etiquette when it comes to soup. When you think about scooping, spilling, and stains, it makes sense [~~scents~~] to scoop the soup from the bowl into the spoon away from you. You find the phrase [~~frase~~] "salt and pepper are married" silly; nevertheless, it helps you to remember that salt and pepper are always passed [~~past~~] together. If you pass the salt, you pass the pepper, too; if you pass the pepper, you pass the salt, too.

| Error Summary | |
| --- | --- |
| **Punctuation:** | |
| Comma | 3 |
| Other | 2 |
| **Spelling** | 3 |

**WEDNESDAY**　　　　　　　　　**WEEK 36**

From the beginning [~~begining~~] of the meal to the end, you don't want to make any [~~no~~] mistakes. At the end of each course, you carefully, quietly, and properly place your used silverware in the position that says, "I'm finished." Thinking of your plate as a clock and your silverware as the hands, you rest the silverware on your [~~you're~~] plate between 3:00 and 6:00. The tips of the silverware are in the center of the plate, the handle ends are at the edge [~~edged~~] of the plate. You are done, and you used good manners.

| Error Summary | |
| --- | --- |
| **Capitalization** | 1 |
| **Language Usage** | 2 |
| **Punctuation:** | |
| Comma | 3 |
| Period | 1 |
| Other | 1 |
| **Spelling** | 2 |

**THURSDAY**　　　　　　　　　**WEEK 36**

Name _____

The phrase "As I send my ship to sea, I sip my soup away from me" helps you remember proper etiquette when it comes to soup. When you think about scooping spilling, and stains it makes scents to scoop the soup from the bowl into the spoon away from you. You find the frase "salt and pepper are married" silly nevertheless, it helps you to remember that salt and pepper are always past together. If you pass the salt, you pass the pepper, too if you pass the pepper, you pass the salt, too.

WATCH FOR
• special words in quotes
• semicolons

**WEDNESDAY**                                    **WEEK 36**

---

From the begining of the meal to the end you don't want to make no mistakes. At the end of each course you carefully, quietly, and properly place your used silverware in the position that says, "I'm finished" Thinking of your plate as a clock and your silverware as the hands, You rest the silverware on you're plate between 3:00 and 6:00. The tips of the silverware are in the center of the plate the handle ends are at the edged of the plate. You are done and you used good manners.

WATCH FOR
• special words in quotes
• semicolons

**THURSDAY**                                    **WEEK 36**

Write one or two paragraphs on the history of chewing gum. If you like, you may include a few lines on how much gum you chew and the reasons why. Begin with one of the following topic sentences, or write your own:

- Have you ever wondered where chewing gum comes from?

- There is a long and interesting history to chewing gum.

- Gum chewing is an activity that has been going on for centuries.

**FRIDAY – WEEK 1**                                    **Science Article: A Sticky Business**

In one or two paragraphs, describe what scurvy is and who was afflicted. Give directions on how to prevent scurvy. Begin with one of the following topic sentences, or write your own:

- Have you eaten an orange today?

- Scurvy is a disease caused by a lack of vitamin C.

- Once a common and fatal disease of sailors, scurvy is easily prevented.

**FRIDAY – WEEK 2**                                                   **Science Article: Scurvy**

In one or two paragraphs, describe some of the people and animals James Herriot writes about in his book *All Creatures Great and Small*. Begin with one of the following topic sentences, or write your own:

- In his book *All Creatures Great and Small*, James Herriot describes all sorts of people and their animals.

- Throughout his veterinary career, James Herriot met a great number of interesting animals and people.

**FRIDAY – WEEK 3**                                    **Book Review:** *All Creatures Great and Small*

Write one or two paragraphs on John Colter. Describe how he became a "mountain man" and what types of things he saw. Begin with one of the following sentences, or write your own:

- John Colter first went west with the explorers Lewis and Clark.

- A grand adventurer, John Colter saw many strange things in his life.

- Throughout his travels, John Colter was witness to great oddities of nature.

As Jane or Edward, respond to your sister Narcissa's letter. Will you join Narcissa at the mission? Why or why not? Are there other family members to consider? Will your brother or sister make the journey with you? Do you want more information? What would you expect to do at the mission? Don't forget to include a date at the beginning of the letter, and to use capital letters and commas correctly in the salutation and closing of your letter.

In one or two paragraphs, explain how skydivers can catch up to each other in the air. Explain what terminal velocity is. Mention acceleration and drag, as well as leg and arm position. Begin with one of the following topic sentences, or write your own:

- Skydivers can catch up to each other in the air by changing their terminal velocity.

- As unlikely as it seems, skydivers do have some control over the speed of their fall.

Write one or two paragraphs on Moses Harris and his tall tale about the petrified valley he found. Explain what it means when something becomes petrified. You may begin with one of the following topic sentences, or write your own:

- Tall tales often have a bit of truth in them.

- Moses Harris, a mountain man, once told a great story about a strange place he found in South Dakota.

In one or two paragraphs, describe Peru's new museum and what it houses. Begin with one of the following topic sentences, or write your own:

- A new museum recently opened in Peru.

- The article "Peru Devotes Museum to 'Tutankhamen of Americas'" describes Peru's new museum.

- The Lord of Sipan has now been buried twice.

This story was fictional, but it was written in a realistic, or believable, style. Continue using this style to write one or two paragraphs describing what happens to Eduardo in the near or distant future. Begin with one of the following sentences, or write your own:

- Even though there was only one month remaining in the school year, Eduardo's parents made him enroll at the new school.

- "Bad news about the baseball team," Eduardo's teacher announced to the class.

Write a one- or two-paragraph letter to a friend. In your letter, mention some of the things you have learned about Greenland from your pen pal Eric. After your date and salutation, you may begin your letter with one of these topic sentences, or write your own:

- Do you know the name of the world's largest island?

- Greenland sure has a lot of ice.

- My pen pal Eric comes from Greenland.

Write one or two paragraphs describing this city of mystery. Begin with one of the following topic sentences, or write your own:

- Archaeologists, detectives of the past, are trying to answer questions about a city of mystery.

- Ancient ruins can be a mystery, but some answers can be found by digging up the past.

- There are some spectacular ruins in Mexico that archaeologists want to know more about.

Write one or two paragraphs to finish this tale. Describe what happens when Pandora opens the chest and allows the evils Sorrow, Pain, Greed, Illness, and a host of others to enter the world. Describe her feelings when she learns that Hope is still left at the very bottom of the chest.

Your mystery vacation was to the country of Chile. Write one or two paragraphs describing what one might see and do in Chile. Begin with one of the following topic sentences, or write your own:

- Visitors to Chile can experience a wide range of activities and landscapes.

- Chile may be one of the best vacation spots in the world.

- Chile is a fascinating country with amazing variety.

In one or two paragraphs, describe some of the things that made Shackleton a great leader. You might want to consider his big dreams, sense of responsibility, and character. Begin with one of the following topic sentences, or write your own:

- Sir Ernest Shackleton possessed all the traits of a good leader.

- Sir Ernest Shackleton knew that a good leader had to have more than big dreams.

- Sir Ernest Shackleton understood leadership.

Decide whether you agree with having soda and candy machines at schools. Write one or two paragraphs stating and supporting your views. Begin with one of the following topic sentences, or write your own:

- Soda and candy machines do not belong at school for a variety of reasons.

- Students are taught to make choices, and I believe they can make their own choices about soda and candy.

Choose a new month and write your own diary entry. You may write an entry for Kitty, or you may write an entry for someone else. If you choose to be someone else, make sure that it is still 1828! Include information about the weather or special activities that might be taking place during that month. Do you like this time of year? Do you like the activities you are involved in? If you can, include one or more sentences of dialog in your diary entry.

**FRIDAY – WEEK 16**                                    **Journal Entries: Kitty's Diary**

Write one or two paragraphs on rules for safe surfing on the Internet. Begin with one of the following topic sentences, or write your own:

- There are several safety rules you should follow while surfing the Internet.

- Safety precautions are necessary, even on the Internet.

- What can you do to surf safely on the Internet?

**FRIDAY – WEEK 17**                                    **Science Article: Safe Surfing**

In one or two paragraphs, discuss atmospheric pressure and its effect on cooking. Begin with one of the following topic sentences, or write your own:

- Cooking at sea level is different from cooking high on a mountain.

- It is important to consider atmospheric pressure when it comes to cooking times.

- Boiling water doesn't always have the same temperature.

**FRIDAY – WEEK 18**                                    **Science Article: High-Altitude Cooking**

Write one or two paragraphs that describe Marian Anderson and what she is known for today. You may begin with one of the following topic sentences, or write your own:

- Marian Anderson's life story is an inspiration for all Americans.

- Marian Anderson overcame many hardships to become a world-class singer.

- Marian Anderson made a difference in the struggle to end racial discrimination.

Write one or two paragraphs describing manatees to someone who wants to learn about them. Begin with one of the following topic sentences, or write your own:

- The manatee is a mammal that lives in the ocean.

- The manatee is a fascinating creature that has been around for millions of years.

- A manatee is a curious creature that lives in the sea.

In one or two paragraphs, describe some of the author's experiences while serving as a Peace Corps volunteer. Begin with one of the following topic sentences, or write your own:

- One Peace Corps volunteer will never forget her time in Belize.

- Interesting things can happen to Peace Corps volunteers.

- When one Peace Corps volunteer was sent to Belize, she had some great adventures.

Write a short diary entry commenting on what you have seen, learned, or done while living at Hull House. After you write your date and salutation, you may begin with one of the following topic sentences, or write your own:

- Today I went to the public playground that Jane Addams started.

- Mama had never heard of such a thing as public baths.

- Miss Addams is a lady, but she still lives with us at Hull House.

**FRIDAY – WEEK 22**                    **Journal Entries: Hull House Diary**

Write one or two paragraphs describing Pecos Bill. Continue writing in the "tall tale" style, adding humor and exaggeration as you like. Begin with one of the following topic sentences, or write your own:

- Pecos Bill was a Texas wrangler.

- Pecos Bill was no ordinary cowpuncher.

- There is only one man alive who has ever ridden a twister.

**FRIDAY – WEEK 23**                                    **Tall Tale: Pecos Bill**

In one or two paragraphs, describe how duct tape can be used to remove warts. Begin with one of the following topic sentences, or write your own:

- In the article "Handyman's Hero Hailed as a Healer," a new method of removing warts is discussed.

- According to the article "Handyman's Hero Hailed as a Healer," there is a new use for duct tape.

- Duct tape may become a doctor's standard tool.

**FRIDAY – WEEK 24**                        **News Article: Duct Tape and Warts**

The Parthenon is an amazing piece of architecture. In one or two paragraphs, describe a piece of architecture that you have seen. The piece of architecture you choose to describe may be big or small. It can be a school, house, museum, tower, bridge, or any other structure. Describe your structure's purpose, the materials used in its construction, its appearance, and its age.

Write one or two paragraphs describing the life Bilal leads and some of the things he knows and sees. Begin with one of the following topic sentences, or write your own:

- As a slave boy in the West African empire of Mali, Bilal worked hard and saw many interesting things.

- Bilal was a boy who saw the famed city of Tombouctu.

- Bilal was a boy who probably knew more about camels than people.

Write one or two paragraphs on the International Space Station. You may begin with one of the following topic sentences, or write your own:

- The International Space Station (ISS) is a true international project.

- Sixteen countries are involved in building a science lab in space.

- The permanent International Space Station has changed the way we explore space.

In one or two paragraphs, briefly describe some of the characters found in <u>The Book of Three</u>. Begin with one of the following topic sentences, or write your own:

- There are several interesting characters in Lloyd Alexander's <u>The Book of Three</u>.

- Lloyd Alexander's cast of characters in <u>The Book of Three</u> is a mixed bunch.

Write one or two paragraphs describing the U.S. courts. You might want to mention the difference between state and federal courts, civil and criminal trials, and the appeal process. Begin with one of the following topic sentences, or write your own:

- In the United States, there are state and federal courts.

- The United States has a court system in which there are different types of courts and cases.

- The United States court system has different levels.

Write one or two paragraphs discussing coed competitive sports. You may agree or disagree with having boys and girls compete together in sports. Use one of these topic sentences, or write your own:

- There are pros and cons when it comes to coed competitive sports.

- I firmly believe that students will be better prepared for life with coed competitive sports.

- School is a time for education, not competitive sports.

Rewrite a paragraph or two of this narrative from the perspective of one of the children. Begin with one of the following topic sentences, or write your own:

- We wanted to go to the beach, but my mother forced us to go bird-watching.

- I usually don't like it when my mother takes us bird-watching.

- My mom is the bird-watcher, but there was one time when I think I was more interested in the outing than she was!

Write several lines of your own interview with Dr. Spark in which he explains the 24-hour clock and why he believes it should be used. Begin with one of the following questions, or write your own:

- "Dr. Spark, I'd like you to explain what you mean by a 24-hour clock."

- "Is 1:00 early morning or early afternoon? Dr. Spark, please explain how there can be no question with the 24-hour clock."

The Apollo 13 mission was declared a "successful failure." Write a paragraph describing what made the Apollo 13 mission a "successful failure." Begin with one of these topic sentences, or write your own:

- The Apollo 13 mission did not reach the moon, but it was still considered a success.

- Sometimes a failure can be turned into a success.

Using the same voice as the previous writer, write one or two paragraphs that describe some of the things Marco Polo saw and the reaction of his neighbors. Begin with one of the following topic sentences, or write your own:

- Marco Polo returned recently from a 24-year adventure.

- Marco Polo claims to have seen many things during his journeys.

- I could listen all day to Marco Polo's stories about his travels.

**FRIDAY – WEEK 34**                    **Historical Fiction: Marco Polo's Tales**

Write one or two paragraphs describing Madagascar. Begin with one of the following topic sentences, or write your own:

- Madagascar is filled with wonderful things to see.

- Although it's just off the coast of Africa, the island of Madagascar is a world of its own.

- Madagascar is a fascinating country filled with many unique creatures and plants.

**FRIDAY – WEEK 35**                    **Description: Madagascar: A Remote Paradise**

In one or two paragraphs, provide some directions for proper dining etiquette. Begin with one of the following topic sentences, or write your own:

- There are some easy rules that help you to remember your manners at the dinner table.

- Need help remembering dining etiquette?

- Good dining manners are easy if you follow some basic directions.

**FRIDAY – WEEK 36**                    **Instructions: Dining Directions**

# Language Handbook

## Basic Rules for Writing and Editing

=== **Contents** ===

EMC 2729 • Daily Paragraph Editing • ©2004 by Evan-Moor Corp.

# Capital Letters

A word that starts with a **capital letter** is special in some way.

Always use a **capital letter** to begin:

| | |
|---|---|
| the first word of a sentence: | Today is the first day of school. |
| the first word of a quotation: | She said, "Today is the first day of school." |
| the salutation (greeting) and closing in a letter: | Dear Grandma,<br>Thanks so much for the birthday gift!<br>Love,<br>Sherry |
| the names of days, months, and holidays: | The fourth Thursday in November is Thanksgiving. |
| people's first and last names, their initials, and their titles: | Mrs. Cruz and her son Felix were both seen by Dr. S. C. Lee.<br><br>**Note:** Many titles can be abbreviated. Use these abbreviations only when you also use the person's name:<br><br>**Mr.** a man     **Capt.** a captain<br>**Mrs.** a married woman     **Lt.** a lieutenant<br>**Ms.** a woman     **Pres.** the president of a country<br>**Dr.** a doctor                    or an organization |
| a word that is used as a name: | I went with Dad and Aunt Terry to visit Grandma.<br><br>**Be Careful!** Do not use a capital letter at the beginning of a word when it is not used as someone's name:<br><br>I went with my dad and my aunt to visit my grandma.<br><br>**Hint:** If you can replace the word with a name, it needs a capital letter:<br>I went with <u>Dad</u>. ⟶ I went with <u>Joe</u>. |
| the word that names yourself - **I**: | My family and **I** enjoy camping together. |

| the names of nationalities and languages: | Mexican, Cuban, and Nicaraguan people all speak Spanish. |
|---|---|
| the names of racial, ethnic, or cultural groups: | There were Asian, Native American, and African dancers at the festival. |
| the names of ships, planes, and space vehicles: | The president flew on <u>Air Force One</u> to see the <u>USS Abraham Lincoln</u>, a U.S. Navy aircraft carrier.<br><br>**Note:** You must also underline the name of a ship, plane, or space vehicle: the space shuttle <u>Columbia</u> |

| to begin the names of these special places and things: | |
|---|---|
| • street names: | Palm Avenue, Cypress Street, Pine Boulevard |
| • cities, states, and countries: | Los Angeles, California, United States of America, Paris, France |
| • continents: | Asia, Europe, South America |
| • landforms and bodies of water: | Great Plains, San Francisco Bay, Great Salt Lake |
| • buildings, monuments, and public places: | the White House, the Statue of Liberty, Yellowstone National Park |
| • historic events: | The Gold Rush began in 1849.<br>The Civil War ended in 1865. |

| titles of books, stories, poems, and magazines: | The story "The Friendly Fruit Bat" appeared in <u>Ranger Rick</u> magazine and in a science book called <u>Flying Mammals</u>. |
|---|---|
| | **Be Careful!** Do not use a capital letter at the beginning of a small word in a title, such as **a**, **an**, **at**, **for**, **in**, and **the**, unless it is the first word in the title. |
| | **Note:** When you write a title, remember . . . |
| | Some titles are underlined: |
| |     **Book Titles:** <u>Frog and Toad</u> |
| |     **Magazine Titles:** <u>Ranger Rick</u> |
| |     **Movie Titles:** <u>Bambi</u> |
| |     **TV Shows:** <u>Sesame Street</u> |
| |     **Newspapers:** <u>The Daily News</u> |
| | Some titles go inside quotation marks: |
| |     **Story Titles:** "The Fox and the Crow" |
| |     **Chapter Titles:** "In Which Piglet Meets a Heffalump" |
| |     **Poem Titles:** "My Shadow" |
| |     **Song Titles:** "Twinkle, Twinkle, Little Star" |
| |     **Titles of Articles:** "Ship Sinks in Bay" |

# Punctuation Marks

**Punctuation** gives information that helps you understand a sentence.

### End Punctuation

Every sentence must end with one of these three punctuation marks: **. ! ?**

A **period** (**.**) shows that a sentence is:

| giving information: | I love to read short stories. |
|---|---|
| giving a mild command: | Choose a short story to read aloud. |
| | **Note:** A period is also used in: |
| | • abbreviations of months and days: Jan. (January), Feb. (February), Mon. (Monday), etc. |
| | • abbreviations of measurements: ft. (foot/feet), in. (inch/inches), lb./lbs. (pound/pounds), oz. (ounce/ounces) |
| | • time: 8:00 a.m., 4:30 p.m., etc. |

A **question mark** (**?**) shows that a sentence is:

| asking a question: | Did you choose a story to read**?** |
|---|---|

An **exclamation point** (**!**) shows that a sentence is:

| expressing strong feelings: | Wow**!** That story is really long**!** |
|---|---|

## Comma

A **comma** (**,**) can help you know how to read things. Commas are often used in sentences. Sometimes commas are used with words or phrases.

Some commas are used to keep things separate. Use a **comma** to separate:

| the name of a city from the name of a state: | El Paso, Texas |
|---|---|
| the name of a city from the name of a country: | London, England |
| the date from the year: | October 12, 2004 |
| the salutation (greeting) from the body of a letter: | Dear Ms. Silver, |
| the closing in a letter from the signature: | Yours truly, |
| two adjectives that tell about the same noun: | Nico is a witty, smart boy.<br><br>**Hint:** To see if you need a comma between two adjectives, use these two "tests":<br><br>**1** Switch the order of the adjectives. If the sentence still makes sense, you must use a comma:<br><br>**YES:** Nico is a witty, smart boy. ⟶ Nico is a smart, witty boy.<br><br>**NO:** Nico has dark brown hair. ⟶ Nico has brown dark hair.<br><br>**2** Put the word "and" between the two adjectives. If the sentence still makes sense, you must use a comma:<br><br>**YES:** Nico is a witty, smart boy. ⟶ Nico is a witty and smart boy.<br><br>**NO:** Nico has dark brown hair. ⟶ Nico has dark and brown hair. |

*Punctuation Marks* (*continued*)

Some commas help you know where to pause when you read a sentence. Use a **comma** to show a pause:

| | |
|---|---|
| between three or more items in a list or series: | Nico won't eat beets, spinach, or shrimp. |
| after or before the name of a person that someone is talking to in a sentence: | **After:**  Nico, I think that you need to eat more.<br>**Before:** I think that you need to eat more, Nico.<br>**Both:**   I think, Nico, that you need to eat more. |
| between the words spoken by someone and the rest of the sentence: | Mrs. Flores said, "It's time to break the piñata now!"<br>"I know," answered Maya. |
| after an exclamation at the beginning of a sentence: | Boy, that's a lot of candy! |
| after a short introductory phrase or clause that comes before the main idea: | After all that candy, nobody was hungry for cake. |
| before and after a word or words that interrupt the main idea of a sentence: | The cake, however, was already out on the picnic table. |
| before and after a word or phrase that renames or gives more information about the noun before it: | The cake, which had thick chocolate frosting, melted in the hot sun.<br>Mrs. Lutz, our neighbor, gave Mom the recipe. |
| before the connecting word in a compound sentence: | The frosting was melted, but the cake was great.<br>**Note:** A simple sentence always includes a <u>subject</u> and a <u>verb</u>, and it expresses a complete thought. A compound sentence joins two simple sentences together, so each of the two parts of a compound sentence has its own <u>subject</u> and <u>verb</u>. The two parts of a compound sentence are joined by a comma and a conjunction. The conjunctions **and**, **but**, **for**, **nor**, **or**, **so**, and **yet** are all used to join two simple sentences into one compound sentence. In a compound sentence, always place the comma before the connecting conjunction:<br><u>Maya</u> <u>ate</u> candy, **but** <u>she</u> <u>was</u> too full to eat cake.<br><u>Nico</u> <u>ate</u> candy, **and** <u>he</u> also <u>ate</u> a piece of cake.<br><u>Nico</u> <u>is</u> thin, **yet** <u>he</u> <u>eats</u> lots of sweets.<br><u>Maya</u> <u>is</u> chubby, **so** <u>she</u> <u>watches</u> what she eats. |

## Semicolon

You can also use a **semicolon** (;) to join two simple sentences.

| You may use a semicolon instead of a period to join two simple sentences: | The party ended at 4:00; the guests left by 4:15. |
|---|---|
| You may use a semicolon instead of a comma: | The party was lots of fun; however, the cleanup was lots of work!<br><br>**Be Careful!** When you use a semicolon instead of a comma, do not use a coordinating conjunction (**and**, **but**, **for**, **nor**, **or**, **so**, **yet**):<br><br>**With a comma:** Maya is responsible, so she wrote her thank-you notes right away.<br><br>**With a semicolon:** Maya is responsible; therefore, she wrote her thank-you notes right away.<br><br>**Note:** Authors may choose to use a semicolon instead of a period or a comma. It depends on the author's style or personal preference, or on the effect the author is trying to achieve in a particular piece of writing. |

## Quotation Marks

Use **quotation marks** (" "):

| before and after words that are spoken by someone: | "This was the best birthday party ever!" Maya said.<br><br>**Note:** Punctuation that follows the speaker's words goes inside the quotation marks:<br>"May I have a piñata at my birthday party?" Martin asked.<br>Mr. Flores replied, "You bet!"<br><br>**Be Careful!** When the words that tell who is speaking come before the quotation, put the comma outside the quotation marks. When the words that tell who is speaking come after the quotation, put the comma inside the quotation marks:<br><br>**Before:** Mrs. Flores asked, "Do you want a chocolate cake, too?"<br>**After:** "I sure do," said Martin. |

| | |
|---|---|
| around words that are being discussed: | The word "piñata" is written with a special letter. |
| around slang or words used in an unusual way: | We all had to "chill out" after the party. |

## Apostrophe

An **apostrophe** ( ' ) helps show who owns something. You add an apostrophe after the name of an owner.

| | |
|---|---|
| When there is just one owner, add an apostrophe first and then add an **S**: | cat + 's ⟶ cat's  The cat's dish was empty. |
| When there is more than one owner, add an **S** first and then add an apostrophe: | cats + ' ⟶ cats'  All the cats' cages at the shelter were nice and big.<br><br>**Be Careful!** When the name of more than one owner does not end with an **S**, add an apostrophe first and then add an **S**:<br><br>children + 's ⟶ children's<br>    The children's cat was in the last cage.<br><br>people + 's ⟶ people's<br>    Other people's pets were making lots of noise. |
| Use an apostrophe when you put two words together to make one word. This is called a contraction. In a contraction, the apostrophe takes the place of the missing letter or letters: | I + am = I'm             do + not = don't<br>you + are = you're        does + not = doesn't<br>he + is = he's            are + not = aren't<br>it + is = it's            could + not = couldn't<br>we + would = we'd         have + not = haven't<br>they + will = they'll     would + not = wouldn't |

**Hyphen**

Use a **hyphen** (−):

| | |
|---|---|
| between numbers in a fraction: | One-half of the candies had walnuts, and one-quarter had almonds. |
| to join two words that work together to make an adjective before a noun: | It's not easy to find low-fat candy and sugar-free soda. |

# Plurals

A noun names a person, place, or thing. A **plural noun** names more than one person, place, or thing.

| | |
|---|---|
| Add an **s** to make most nouns plural: | girl ⟶ girl + s ⟶ girl**s**<br>river ⟶ river + s ⟶ river**s** |
| If the noun ends in **ch**, **s**, **sh**, or **x**, add **es**: | lunch ⟶ lunch + es ⟶ lunch**es**<br>dress ⟶ dress + es ⟶ dress**es**<br>brush ⟶ brush + es ⟶ brush**es**<br>fox ⟶ fox + es ⟶ fox**es** |
| If the noun ends in **y**, change the y to **i** and add **es**: | fly ⟶ fli + es ⟶ fli**es**<br>story ⟶ stori + es ⟶ stori**es**<br><br>**Note:** If the noun ends in a vowel plus **y**, just add **s**:<br>bay ⟶ bay + s ⟶ bay**s**<br>key ⟶ key + s ⟶ key**s**<br>boy ⟶ boy + s ⟶ boy**s**<br><br>**Be Careful!** Some plural nouns do not have an **s** at all:<br>child ⟶ **children**    foot ⟶ **feet**<br>man ⟶ **men**    tooth ⟶ **teeth**<br>woman ⟶ **women**    goose ⟶ **geese** |